I0281474

MznLnx

Missing Links Exam Preps

Exam Prep for

Sales Force Management

Johnston & Marshall, 8th Edition

The MznLnx Exam Prep is your link from the texbook and lecture to your exams.
The MznLnx Exam Preps are unauthorized and comprehensive reviews of your textbooks.

MznLnx

Rico
Publications

Exam Prep for Sales Force Management
8th Edition
Johnston & Marshall

Publisher: Raymond Houge
Assistant Editor: Michael Rouger
Text and Cover Designer: Lisa Buckner
Marketing Manager: Sara Swagger
Project Manager, Editorial Production: Jerry Emerson
Art Director: Vernon Lowerui

Product Manager: Dave Mason
Editorial Assitant: Rachel Guzmanji
Pedagogy: Debra Long
Cover Image: Jim Reed/Getty Images
Text and Cover Printer: City Printing, Inc.
Compositor: Media Mix, Inc.

Printed in the United States
ISBN:

For more information about our products, contact us at:
Dave.Mason@RicoPublications.com

For permission to use material from this text or product, submit a request online to:
Dave.Mason@RicoPublications.com

Contents

TO THE STUDENT

COMPREHENSIVE

The *MznLnx* Exam Prep series is designed to help you pass your exams. Editors at MznLnx review your textbooks and then prepare these practice exams to help you master the textbook material. Unlike study guides, workbooks, and practice tests provided by the texbook publisher and textbook authors, *MznLnx* gives you ***all*** of the material in each chapter in exam form, not just samples, so you can be sure to nail your exam.

MECHANICAL

The MznLnx Exam Prep series creates exams that will help you learn the subject matter as well as test you on your understanding. Each question is designed to help you master the concept. Just working through the exams, you gain an understanding of the subject--its a simple mechanical process that produces success.

INTEGRATED STUDY GUIDE AND REVIEW

MznLnx is not just a set of exams designed to test you, its also a comprehensive review of the subject content. Each exam question is also a review of the concept, making sure that you will get the answer correct without having to go to other sources of material. You learn as you go! Its the easiest way to pass an exam.

HUMOR

Studying can be tedious and dry. MznLnx's instructional design includes moderate humor within the exam questions on occassion, to break the tedium and revitalize the brain

1. Importance of _________ is critical for any commercial organization. Expanding business is not possible without increasing sales volumes, and effective _________ goal is to organize sales team work in such a manner that ensures a growing flow of regular customers and increasing amount of sales.

The four phase-model of Management Process

1. Conception
2. Planning
3. Execution
4. Control

This model is cyclical, so it is a constant/continuous process.

===_________ is attainment of sales force goals in a effective ' efficient manner through planning, staffing, training, leading ' controlling organizational resources.

a. Sales process
b. Hit rate
c. Request for proposal
d. Sales management

2. _________ is an advertisement in which a particular product specifically mentions a competitor by name for the express purpose of showing why the competitor is inferior to the product naming it.

This should not be confused with parody advertisements, where a fictional product is being advertised for the purpose of poking fun at the particular advertisement, nor should it be confused with the use of a coined brand name for the purpose of comparing the product without actually naming an actual competitor. ('Wikipedia tastes better and is less filling than the Encyclopedia Galactica.')

In the 1980s, during what has been referred to as the cola wars, soft-drink manufacturer Pepsi ran a series of advertisements where people, caught on hidden camera, in a blind taste test, chose Pepsi over rival Coca-Cola.

a. Cost per conversion
b. GL-70
c. Heavy-up
d. Comparative advertising

3. A _________ is a business that is independently owned and operated, with a small number of employees and relatively low volume of sales. The legal definition of 'small' often varies by country and industry, but is generally under 100 employees in the United States and under 50 employees in the European Union. In comparison, the definition of mid-sized business by the number of employees is generally under 500 in the U.S. and 250 for the European Union.

a. Small Business
b. Product support
c. Customer centricity
d. Time to market

4. The _________ is a United States government agency that provides support to small businesses.

The mission of the _________ is 'to maintain and strengthen the nation's economy by enabling the establishment and viability of small businesses and by assisting in the economic recovery of communities after disasters.'

The _________ makes loans directly to businesses and acts as a guarantor on bank loans. In some circumstances it also makes loans to victims of natural disasters, works to get government procurement contracts for small businesses, and assists businesses with management, technical and training issues.

a. 6-3-5 Brainwriting
b. Power III
c. 180SearchAssistant
d. Small Business Administration

5. _________ is defined by the American _________ Association as the activity, set of institutions, and processes for creating, communicating, delivering, and exchanging offerings that have value for customers, clients, partners, and society at large. The term developed from the original meaning which referred literally to going to market, as in shopping, or going to a market to sell goods or services.

_________ practice tends to be seen as a creative industry, which includes advertising, distribution and selling.

a. Marketing
b. Customer acquisition management
c. Product naming
d. Marketing myopia

6. In environmental modeling and especially in hydrology, a _________ model means a model that is acceptably consistent with observed natural processes, i.e. that simulates well, for example, observed river discharge. It is a key concept of the so-called Generalized Likelihood Uncertainty Estimation (GLUE) methodology to quantify how uncertain environmental predictions are.

a. 180SearchAssistant
b. 6-3-5 Brainwriting
c. Power III
d. Behavioral

7. _________ is a sub-discipline and type of marketing. There are two main definitional characteristics which distinguish it from other types of marketing. The first is that it attempts to send its messages directly to consumers, without the use of intervening media.

a. Direct Marketing Associations
b. Database marketing
c. Direct marketing
d. Power III

8. _________ is subcontracting a process, such as product design or manufacturing, to a third-party company. The decision to outsource is often made in the interest of lowering cost or making better use of time and energy costs, redirecting or conserving energy directed at the competencies of a particular business, or to make more efficient use of land, labor, capital, (information) technology and resources. _________ became part of the business lexicon during the 1980s.

a. Outsourcing
b. In-house
c. Intangible assets
d. ACNielsen

9. Sales force management systems are information systems used in marketing and management that help automate some sales and sales force management functions. They are frequently combined with a marketing information system, in which case they are often called Customer Relationship Management (CRM) systems.

_________ Systems , typically a part of a company's customer relationship management system, is a system that automatically records all the stages in a sales process.

a. Power III
b. 180SearchAssistant
c. 6-3-5 Brainwriting
d. Sales force automation

10. A _________ is the space, actual or metaphorical, in which a market operates. The term is also used in a trademark law context to denote the actual consumer environment, ie. the 'real world' in which products and services are provided and consumed.

a. Marketplace
b. Power III
c. 6-3-5 Brainwriting
d. 180SearchAssistant

11. _________ is a branch of philosophy which seeks to address questions about morality, such as how a moral outcome can be achieved in a specific situation (applied _________), how moral values should be determined (normative _________), what moral values people actually abide by (descriptive _________), what the fundamental semantic, ontological, and epistemic nature of _________ or morality is (meta-_________), and how moral capacity or moral agency develops and what its nature is (moral psychology.)

Socrates was one of the first Greek philosophers to encourage both scholars and the common citizen to turn their attention from the outside world to the condition of man. In this view, Knowledge having a bearing on human life was placed highest, all other knowledge being secondary.

a. AMAX
b. ACNielsen
c. ADTECH
d. Ethics

12. In economic models, the _________ time frame assumes no fixed factors of production. Firms can enter or leave the marketplace, and the cost (and availability) of land, labor, raw materials, and capital goods can be assumed to vary. In contrast, in the short-run time frame, certain factors are assumed to be fixed, because there is not sufficient time for them to change.
a. Power III
b. 6-3-5 Brainwriting
c. 180SearchAssistant
d. Long-run

13. Procter is a surname, and may also refer to:

- Bryan Waller Procter (pseud. Barry Cornwall), English poet
- Goodwin Procter, American law firm
- _________, consumer products multinational

.

a. Flyer
b. Procter ' Gamble
c. Convergent
d. Black PRies

14. _________ is systematic determination of merit, worth, and significance of something or someone using criteria against a set of standards. _________ often is used to characterize and appraise subjects of interest in a wide range of human enterprises, including the arts, criminal justice, foundations and non-profit organizations, government, health care, and other human services.

Depending on the topic of interest, there are professional groups which look to the quality and rigor of the _________ process.

a. ACNielsen
b. ADTECH
c. AMAX
d. Evaluation

15. _________ is the state or fact of exclusive rights and control over property, which may be an object, land/real estate, or some other kind of property (like government-granted monopolies collectively referred to as intellectual property.) It is embodied in an _________ right also referred to as title.

_________ is the key building block in the development of the capitalist socio-economic system.

a. AMAX
b. Ownership
c. ACNielsen
d. ADTECH

16. _________ is the process of approaching prospective customers or clients, typically via telephone, who were not expecting such an interaction. The word 'cold' is used because the person receiving the call is not expecting a call or has not specifically asked to be contacted by a sales person.

Within the United Kingdom, the Privacy and Electronic Communications (EC Directive) Regulations 2003 make it unlawful to transmit an automated recorded message for direct marketing purposes via a telephone, without prior consent of the subscriber.

a. Power III
b. Database marketing
c. Direct Marketing Associations
d. Cold calling

17. _________ is a method of direct marketing in which a salesperson solicits to prospective customers to buy products or services, either over the phone or through a subsequent face to face or Web conferencing appointment scheduled during the call.

_________ can also include recorded sales pitches programmed to be played over the phone via automatic dialing. _________ has come under fire in recent years, being viewed as an annoyance by many.

a. Phishing
b. Directory Harvest Attack
c. Joe job
d. Telemarketing

18. _________ refers to the structured transmission of data between organizations by electronic means. It is used to transfer electronic documents from one computer system to another (ie) from one trading partner to another trading partner. It is more than mere E-mail; for instance, organizations might replace bills of lading and even checks with appropriate _________ messages.
a. ADTECH
b. ACNielsen
c. AMAX
d. Electronic data interchange

19. _________ is a broad label that refers to any individuals or households that use goods and services generated within the economy. The concept of a _________ is used in different contexts, so that the usage and significance of the term may vary.

A _________ is a person who uses any product or service.

a. 180SearchAssistant
b. 6-3-5 Brainwriting
c. Power III
d. Consumer

20. _________ refer to a collection of facts usually collected as the result of experience, observation or experiment or a set of premises. This may consist of numbers, words particularly as measurements or observations of a set of variables. _________ are often viewed as a lowest level of abstraction from which information and knowledge are derived.

a. Mean
b. Sample size
c. Pearson product-moment correlation coefficient
d. Data

21. _________ is the difference between the revenues earned from and the costs associated with the customer relationship in a specified period.

According to Philip Kotler,'a profitable customer is a person, household or a company that overtime, yields a revenue stream that exceeds by an acceptable amount the company's cost stream of attracting, selling and servicing the customer'

Although _________ is nothing more than the result of applying the business concept of profit to a customer relationship, measuring the profitability of a firm's customers or customer groups can often deliver useful business insights.

Quite often a very small percentage of the firm's best customers will account for a large portion of firm profit.

a. Power III
b. 180SearchAssistant
c. Customer profitability
d. Cost management

22. _________ is difficult to define. For example, in 1952, Alfred Kroeber and Clyde Kluckhohn compiled a list of 164 definitions of '_________' in _________: A Critical Review of Concepts and Definitions. However, the word '_________' is most commonly used in three basic senses:

- excellence of taste in the fine arts and humanities
- an integrated pattern of human knowledge, belief, and behavior that depends upon the capacity for symbolic thought and social learning
- the set of shared attitudes, values, goals, and practices that characterizes an institution, organization or group.

When the concept first emerged in eighteenth- and nineteenth-century Europe, it connoted a process of cultivation or improvement, as in agriculture or horticulture. In the nineteenth century, it came to refer first to the betterment or refinement of the individual, especially through education, and then to the fulfillment of national aspirations or ideals.

a. Albert Einstein
b. African Americans
c. Culture
d. AStore

23. _________ is a measure of the strength of a brand, product, service relative to competitive offerings. There is often a geographic element to the competitive landscape. In defining _________, you must see to what extent a product, brand, or firm controls a product category in a given geographic area.
a. Discretionary spending
b. Market dominance
c. Productivity
d. Market system

24. A _________ is a plan of action designed to achieve a particular goal.

_________ is different from tactics. In military terms, tactics is concerned with the conduct of an engagement while _________ is concerned with how different engagements are linked.

a. 6-3-5 Brainwriting
b. Strategy
c. 180SearchAssistant
d. Power III

25. A personal and cultural _________ is a relative ethic _________, an assumption upon which implementation can be extrapolated. A _________ system is a set of consistent _________s and measures that is soo not true. A principle _________ is a foundation upon which other _________s and measures of integrity are based.
a. Perceptual maps
b. Package-on-Package
c. Value
d. Supreme Court of the United States

26. _________ LLP, based in Chicago, was once one of the 'Big Five' accounting firms among PricewaterhouseCoopers, Deloitte Touche Tohmatsu, Ernst ' Young and KPMG, providing auditing, tax, and consulting services to large corporations. In 2002, the firm voluntarily surrendered its licenses to practice as Certified Public Accountants in the United States after being found guilty of criminal charges relating to the firm's handling of the auditing of Enron, the energy corporation, resulting in the loss of 85,000 jobs. Although the verdict was subsequently overturned by the Supreme Court of the United States, it has not returned as a viable business.

a. ADTECH
b. Arthur Andersen
c. ACNielsen
d. AMAX

27. _________ is a form of communication that typically attempts to persuade potential customers to purchase or to consume more of a particular brand of product or service. 'While now central to the contemporary global economy and the reproduction of global production networks, it is only quite recently that _________ has been more than a marginal influence on patterns of sales and production. The formation of modern _________ was intimately bound up with the emergence of new forms of monopoly capitalism around the end of the 19th and beginning of the 20th century as one element in corporate strategies to create, organize and where possible control markets, especially for mass produced consumer goods.
a. Advertising
b. ADTECH
c. ACNielsen
d. AMAX

28. In economics, an externality or spillover of an economic transaction is an impact on a party that is not directly involved in the transaction. In such a case, prices do not reflect the full costs or benefits in production or consumption of a product or service. A positive impact is called an _________ benefit, while a negative impact is called an _________ cost.
a. AMAX
b. ACNielsen
c. ADTECH
d. External

29. _________ is the realization of an application idea, model, design, specification, standard, algorithm an _________ is a realization of a technical specification or algorithm as a program, software component, or other computer system. Many _________s may exist for a given specification or standard.
a. ACNielsen
b. AMAX
c. ADTECH
d. Implementation

30. Electronic commerce, commonly known as _________ or eCommerce, consists of the buying and selling of products or services over electronic systems such as the Internet and other computer networks. The amount of trade conducted electronically has grown extraordinarily with wide-spread Internet usage. A wide variety of commerce is conducted in this way, spurring and drawing on innovations in electronic funds transfer, supply chain management, Internet marketing, online transaction processing, electronic data interchange (EDI), inventory management systems, and automated data collection systems.

a. ADTECH
b. ACNielsen
c. E-commerce
d. AMAX

31. A _________ is a process that can allow an organization to concentrate its limited resources on the greatest opportunities to increase sales and achieve a sustainable competitive advantage. A _________ should be centered around the key concept that customer satisfaction is the main goal.

A _________ is most effective when it is an integral component of corporate strategy, defining how the organization will successfully engage customers, prospects, and competitors in the market arena.

a. Psychographic
b. Societal marketing
c. Cyberdoc
d. Marketing strategy

32. _________ or _________ data refers to selected population characteristics as used in government, marketing or opinion research, or the _________ profiles used in such research. Note the distinction from the term 'demography' Commonly-used _________ include race, age, income, disabilities, mobility (in terms of travel time to work or number of vehicles available), educational attainment, home ownership, employment status, and even location.

a. AStore
b. African Americans
c. Albert Einstein
d. Demographic

33. _________s is the social science that studies the production, distribution, and consumption of goods and services. The term _________s comes from the Ancient Greek oá¼°κονομÎ¯α from oá¼¶κος (oikos, 'house') + νÏŒμος (nomos, 'custom' or 'law'), hence 'rules of the house(hold)'. Current _________ models developed out of the broader field of political economy in the late 19th century, owing to a desire to use an empirical approach more akin to the physical sciences.

a. ADTECH
b. Industrial organization
c. Economic
d. ACNielsen

34. _________ is the practice of influencing decisions made by government. It includes all attempts to influence legislators and officials, whether by other legislators, constituents or organized groups. A lobbyist is a person who tries to influence legislation on behalf of a special interest or a member of a lobby.

a. Albert Einstein
b. AStore
c. African Americans
d. Lobbying

35. _________ is the practice of managing the flow of information between an organization and its publics. _________ - often referred to as _________ - gains an organization or individual exposure to their audiences using topics of public interest and news items that do not require direct payment. Because _________ places exposure in credible third-party outlets, it offers a third-party legitimacy that advertising does not have.

a. Symbolic analysis
b. Power III
c. Public relations
d. Graphic communication

36. _________ describes the processes and activities that need to take place to characterise and monitor the quality of the environment. _________ is used in the preparation of environmental impact assessments, as well as in many circumstances in which human activities carry a risk of harmful effects on the natural environment. All monitoring strategies and programmes have reasons and justifications which are often designed to establish the current status of an environment or to establish trends in environmental parameters.

a. Environmental monitoring
b. ADTECH
c. ACNielsen
d. AMAX

37. _________ is one of the four elements of marketing mix. An organization or set of organizations (go-betweens) involved in the process of making a product or service available for use or consumption by a consumer or business user.

The other three parts of the marketing mix are product, pricing, and promotion.

a. Better Living Through Chemistry
b. Japan Advertising Photographers' Association
c. Distribution
d. Comparison-Shopping agent

38. _________, known in the United States as antitrust law, has three main elements:

- prohibiting agreements or practices that restrict free trading and competition between business entities. This includes in particular the repression of cartels.
- banning abusive behaviour by a firm dominating a market, or anti-competitive practices that tend to lead to such a dominant position. Practices controlled in this way may include predatory pricing, tying, price gouging, refusal to deal, and many others.
- supervising the mergers and acquisitions of large corporations, including some joint ventures. Transactions that are considered to threaten the competitive process can be prohibited altogether, or approved subject to 'remedies' such as an obligation to divest part of the merged business or to offer licences or access to facilities to enable other businesses to continue competing.

The substance and practice of _________ varies from jurisdiction to jurisdiction. Protecting the interests of consumers (consumer welfare) and ensuring that entrepreneurs have an opportunity to compete in the market economy are often treated as important objectives. _________ is closely connected with law on deregulation of access to markets, state aids and subsidies, the privatisation of state owned assets and the establishment of independent sector regulators. In recent decades, _________ has been viewed as a way to provide better public services.

a. Covenant not to compete
b. Competition law
c. Right to Financial Privacy Act
d. Denominazione di origine controllata

39. _________ is a form of government regulation which protects the interests of consumers. For example, a government may require businesses to disclose detailed information about products--particularly in areas where safety or public health is an issue, such as food. _________ is linked to the idea of consumer rights (that consumers have various rights as consumers), and to the formation of consumer organizations which help consumers make better choices in the marketplace.

a. Trademark dilution
b. Federal Bureau of Investigation
c. Sound trademark
d. Consumer protection

40. _________ is a sales technique in which a salesperson walks from one door of a house to another trying to sell a product or service to the general public. A variant of this involves cold calling first, when another sales representative attempts to gain agreement that a salesperson should visit. _________ selling is usually conducted in the afternoon hours, when the majority of people are at home.

a. Marketing management
b. Door-to-door
c. Performance-based advertising
d. Fast moving consumer goods

41. The _________ is a US law that applies to labels on many consumer products. It requires the label to state:

- The identity of the product;
- The name and place of business of the manufacturer, packer, or distributor; and
- The net quantity of contents.

The contents statement must include both metric and U.S. customary units.

Passed under Lyndon B. Johnson in 1966, the law first took effect on July 1, 1967. The metric labeling requirement was added in 1992 and took effect on February 14, 1994.

a. 6-3-5 Brainwriting
b. Fair Packaging and Labeling Act
c. Power III
d. 180SearchAssistant

42. The _________ is an independent agency of the United States government, established in 1914 by the _________ Act. Its principal mission is the promotion of 'consumer protection' and the elimination and prevention of what regulators perceive to be harmfully 'anti-competitive' business practices, such as coercive monopoly.

The _________ Act was one of President Wilson's major acts against trusts.

a. 6-3-5 Brainwriting
b. Power III
c. Federal Trade Commission
d. 180SearchAssistant

43. The _________ of 1914 (15 U.S.C Â§Â§ 41-58, as amended) established the Federal Trade Commission (FTC), a bipartisan body of five members appointed by the President of the United States for seven year terms. This Commission was authorized to issue Cease and Desist orders to large corporations to curb unfair trade practices. This Act also gave more flexibility to the US congress for judicial matters.

a. Gripe site
b. Product liability
c. Comparative negligence
d. Federal Trade Commission Act

44. _________ in economics and business is the result of an exchange and from that trade we assign a numerical monetary value to a good, service or asset. If I trade 4 apples for an orange, the _________ of an orange is 4 - apples. Inversely, the _________ of an apple is 1/4 oranges.
a. Pricing
b. Contribution margin-based pricing
c. Discounts and allowances
d. Price

45. _________ exists when sales of identical goods or services are transacted at different prices from the same provider. In a theoretical market with perfect information, no transaction costs or prohibition on secondary exchange (or re-selling) to prevent arbitrage, _________ can only be a feature of monopoly and oligopoly markets, where market power can be exercised. Otherwise, the moment the seller tries to sell the same good at different prices, the buyer at the lower price can arbitrage by selling to the consumer buying at the higher price but with a tiny discount.
a. Resale price maintenance
b. Price
c. Penetration pricing
d. Price discrimination

46. _________ is an agreement between business competitors to sell the same product or service at the same price. In general, it is an agreement intended to ultimately push the price of a product as high as possible, leading to profits for all the sellers. _________ can also involve any agreement to fix, peg, discount or stabilize prices.
a. Price fixing
b. Price competition
c. Non-price competition
d. Direct competition

47. The _________ of 1936 (or Anti-Price Discrimination Act, 15 U.S.C. Â§ 13) is a United States federal law that prohibits what were considered, at the time of passage, to be anticompetitive practices by producers, specifically price discrimination. It grew out of practices in which chain stores were allowed to purchase goods at lower prices than other retailers.

a. Registered trademark symbol
b. Trademark infringement
c. Robinson-Patman Act
d. Fair Debt Collection Practices Act

48. The _________ of 1968 is a United States federal law designed to protect consumers in credit transactions, by requiring clear disclosure of key terms of the lending arrangement and all costs. The statute is contained in Title I of the Consumer Credit Protection Act, as amended (15 U.S.C. Â§ 1601 et seq.).
a. 180SearchAssistant
b. 6-3-5 Brainwriting
c. Truth in Lending Act
d. Power III

49. _________ is a rivalry between individuals, groups, nations for territory, a niche, or allocation of resources. It arises whenever two or more parties strive for a goal which cannot be shared. _________ occurs naturally between living organisms which co-exist in the same environment.
a. Price fixing
b. Non-price competition
c. Price competition
d. Competition

50. _________ is a contract between two parties, one being the employer and the other being the employee. An employee may be defined as: 'A person in the service of another under any contract of hire, express or implied, oral or written, where the employer has the power or right to control and direct the employee in the material details of how the work is to be performed.' Black's Law Dictionary page 471 (5th ed. 1979.)
a. ACNielsen
b. Employment
c. AMAX
d. ADTECH

51. _________ was cofounded in 1994 by Billy Prim and Andrew Filipowski, both North Carolina businessmen, with the goal of building a national brand of propane tank exchange that would capitalize on the growth in gas grill sales and year-round grilling. At the time, propane tank exchange was viewed as a commodity and a large number of consumers got their tanks filled by various vendors.

A national distribution network was constructed and retailer partnerships were established.

a. Factory direct
b. Blue Rhino
c. Wholesale list
d. Teleflorist

52. _________ is the use of governmental powers by government officials for illegitimate private gain. Misuse of government power for other purposes, such as repression of political opponents and general police brutality, is not considered _________. Neither are illegal acts by private persons or corporations not directly involved with the government.
a. Political corruption
b. Albert Einstein
c. AStore
d. African Americans

53. In statistics, an _________ is a term in a statistical model added when the effect of two or more variables is not simply additive. Such a term reflects that the effect of one variable depends on the values of one or more other variables.

Thus, for a response Y and two variables x_1 and x_2 an additive model would be:

$$Y = ax_1 + bx_2 + \text{error}$$

In contrast to this,

$$Y = ax_1 + bx_2 + c(x_1 \times x_2) + \text{error},$$

is an example of a model with an _________ between variables x_1 and x_2 ('error' refers to the random variable whose value by which y differs from the expected value of y.)

a. ADTECH
b. AMAX
c. ACNielsen
d. Interaction

54. _________ is a process of gathering, analyzing, and dispensing information for tactical or strategic purposes. The _________ process entails obtaining both factual and subjective information on the business environments in which a company is operating or considering entering.

There are three ways of scanning the business environment:

- Ad-hoc scanning - Short term, infrequent examinations usually initiated by a crisis
- Regular scanning - Studies done on a regular schedule (say, once a year)
- Continuous scanning(also called continuous learning) - continuous structured data collection and processing on a broad range of environmental factors

Most commentators feel that in today's turbulent business environment the best scanning method available is continuous scanning.This allows the firm to :

-act quickly-take advantage of opportunities before competitors do-respond to environmental threats before significant damage is done

The Macro Environment

_________ usually refers just to the macro environment, but it can also include:-industry -competitor analysis -marketing research(consumer analysis) -New Product Development(product innovations)- the company's internal environment

Macro _________ involves analysing:

- The Economy

GDP per capitaeconomic growthunemployment]] rateinflation]] rateconsumer and investor confidenceinventory levelscurrency exchange ratesmerchandise trade balancefinancial and political health of trading partnersbalance of paymentsfuture trends

- Government

political climate - amount of government activitypolitical stability and riskgovernment debtbudget deficit or surpluscorporate and personal tax ratespayroll taxesimport tariffs and quotasexport restrictionsrestrictions on international financial flows

- Legal

minimum wage lawsenvironmental protection lawsworker safety lawsunion lawscopyright and patent lawsanti- monopoly lawsSunday closing lawsmunicipal licenceslaws that favour business investment

- Technology

efficiency of infrastructure, including: roads, ports, airports, rolling stock, hospitals, education, healthcare, communication, etc.industrial productivitynew manufacturing processesnew products and services of competitorsnew products and services of supply chain partnersany new technology that could impact the companycost and accessibility of electrical power

- Ecology
    - ecological concerns that affect the firms production processes
    - ecological concerns that affect customers' buying habits
    - ecological concerns that affect customers' perception of the company or product
- Socio-Cultural
    - demographic factors such as:
        - population size and distribution
        - age distribution
        - education levels
        - income levels
        - ethnic origins
        - religious affiliations
    - attitudes towards:
        - materialism, capitalism, free enterprise
        - individualism, role of family, role of government, collectivism
        - role of church and religion
        - consumerism
        - environmentalism
        - importance of work, pride of accomplishment
    - cultural structures including:
        - diet and nutrition
        - housing conditions
- Potential Suppliers
    - Labour supply
        - quantity of labour available
        - quality of labour available
        - stability of labour supply
        - wage expectations
        - employee turn-over rate
        - strikes and labour relations
        - educational facilities
    - Material suppliers
        - quality, quantity, price, and stability of material inputs
        - delivery delays
        - proximity of bulky or heavy material inputs
        - level of competition among suppliers
    - Service Providers
        - quantity, quality, price, and stability of service facilitators
        - special requirements
- Stakeholders
    - Lobbyists
    - Shareholders
    - Employees
    - Partners

Scanning these macro environmental variables for threats and opportunities requires that each issue be rated on two dimensions. It must be rated on its potential impact on the company, and rated on its likeliness of occurrence.

a. Environmental scanning
b. AMAX
c. ACNielsen
d. ADTECH

55. The phrase _________, according to the Organization for Economic Co-operation and Development, refers to 'creative work undertaken on a systematic basis in order to increase the stock of knowledge, including knowledge of man, culture and society, and the use of this stock of knowledge to devise new applications [sic]' Though it is questionable that an organization is needed for this definition, as it is quite obvious that _________ refers to the _________ of something.

New product design and development is more often than not a crucial factor in the survival of a company. In an industry that is fast changing, firms must continually revise their design and range of products.

a. 180SearchAssistant
b. Research and development
c. Power III
d. 6-3-5 Brainwriting

56. A _________ or logistics network is the system of organizations, people, technology, activities, information and resources involved in moving a product or service from supplier to customer. _________ activities transform natural resources, raw materials and components into a finished product that is delivered to the end customer. In sophisticated _________ systems, used products may re-enter the _________ at any point where residual value is recyclable.

a. Supply chain network
b. Demand chain management
c. Purchasing
d. Supply chain

57. _________ is the process of estimation in unknown situations. Prediction is a similar, but more general term. Both can refer to estimation of time series, cross-sectional or longitudinal data.

a. Power III
b. 180SearchAssistant
c. Forecasting
d. 6-3-5 Brainwriting

58. Human beings are also considered to be _________ because they have the ability to change raw materials into valuable _________. The term Human _________ can also be defined as the skills, energies, talents, abilities and knowledge that are used for the production of goods or the rendering of services. While taking into account human beings as _________, the following things have to be kept in mind:

- The size of the population
- The capabilities of the individuals in that population

Many _________ cannot be consumed in their original form. They have to be processed in order to change them into more usable commodities.

a. Resources
b. 180SearchAssistant
c. Power III
d. 6-3-5 Brainwriting

59. Organizational culture is not the same as _________. It is wider and deeper concepts, something that an organization 'is' rather than what it 'has' (according to Buchanan and Huczynski.)

_________ is the total sum of the values, customs, traditions and meanings that make a company unique.

a. Power III
b. 180SearchAssistant
c. Cross-functional team
d. Corporate culture

60. _________ is understood as a business unit within the overall corporate identity which is distinguishable from other business because it serves a defined external market where management can conduct strategic planning in relation to products and markets. When companies become really large, they are best thought of as being composed of a number of businesses (or _________s.)

In the broader domain of strategic management, the phrase '_________' came into use in the 1960s, largely as a result of General Electric's many units.

a. Cost leadership
b. Strategic business unit
c. Corporate strategy
d. Business strategy

1. A _________ is a plan of action designed to achieve a particular goal.

_________ is different from tactics. In military terms, tactics is concerned with the conduct of an engagement while _________ is concerned with how different engagements are linked.

a. Power III
b. 180SearchAssistant
c. 6-3-5 Brainwriting
d. Strategy

2. Importance of _________ is critical for any commercial organization. Expanding business is not possible without increasing sales volumes, and effective _________ goal is to organize sales team work in such a manner that ensures a growing flow of regular customers and increasing amount of sales.

The four phase-model of Management Process

1. Conception
2. Planning
3. Execution
4. Control

This model is cyclical, so it is a constant/continuous process.

===_________ is attainment of sales force goals in a effective ' efficient manner through planning, staffing, training, leading ' controlling organizational resources.

a. Request for proposal
b. Sales process
c. Sales management
d. Hit rate

3. _________ is systematic determination of merit, worth, and significance of something or someone using criteria against a set of standards. _________ often is used to characterize and appraise subjects of interest in a wide range of human enterprises, including the arts, criminal justice, foundations and non-profit organizations, government, health care, and other human services.

Depending on the topic of interest, there are professional groups which look to the quality and rigor of the _________ process.

a. ADTECH
b. ACNielsen
c. AMAX
d. Evaluation

4. _________ is a measure of the strength of a brand, product, service relative to competitive offerings. There is often a geographic element to the competitive landscape. In defining _________, you must see to what extent a product, brand, or firm controls a product category in a given geographic area.

a. Productivity
b. Discretionary spending
c. Market dominance
d. Market system

5. In economic models, the _________ time frame assumes no fixed factors of production. Firms can enter or leave the marketplace, and the cost (and availability) of land, labor, raw materials, and capital goods can be assumed to vary. In contrast, in the short-run time frame, certain factors are assumed to be fixed, because there is not sufficient time for them to change.

a. 6-3-5 Brainwriting
b. Long-run
c. Power III
d. 180SearchAssistant

6. _________ is the state or fact of exclusive rights and control over property, which may be an object, land/real estate, or some other kind of property (like government-granted monopolies collectively referred to as intellectual property.) It is embodied in an _________ right also referred to as title.

_________ is the key building block in the development of the capitalist socio-economic system.

a. Ownership
b. ACNielsen
c. ADTECH
d. AMAX

7. A personal and cultural _________ is a relative ethic _________, an assumption upon which implementation can be extrapolated. A _________ system is a set of consistent _________s and measures that is soo not true. A principle _________ is a foundation upon which other _________s and measures of integrity are based.

a. Package-on-Package
b. Supreme Court of the United States
c. Perceptual maps
d. Value

8. Organizational culture is not the same as _________. It is wider and deeper concepts, something that an organization 'is' rather than what it 'has' (according to Buchanan and Huczynski.)

_________ is the total sum of the values, customs, traditions and meanings that make a company unique.

a. Corporate culture
b. 180SearchAssistant
c. Cross-functional team
d. Power III

9. A _________ is a subgroup of people or organizations sharing one or more characteristics that cause them to have similar product and/or service needs. A true _________ meets all of the following criteria: it is distinct from other segments (different segments have different needs), it is homogeneous within the segment (exhibits common needs); it responds similarly to a market stimulus, and it can be reached by a market intervention. The term is also used when consumers with identical product and/or service needs are divided up into groups so they can be charged different amounts.
a. Commercial planning
b. Customer insight
c. Production orientation
d. Market segment

10. A supply chain is the system of organizations, people, technology, activities, information and resources involved in moving a product or service from _________ to customer. Supply chain activities transform natural resources, raw materials and components into a finished product that is delivered to the end customer. In sophisticated supply chain systems, used products may re-enter the supply chain at any point where residual value is recyclable.
a. Rebate
b. Bringin' Home the Oil
c. Product line extension
d. Supplier

11. _________ is difficult to define. For example, in 1952, Alfred Kroeber and Clyde Kluckhohn compiled a list of 164 definitions of '_________' in _________: A Critical Review of Concepts and Definitions. However, the word '_________' is most commonly used in three basic senses:

- excellence of taste in the fine arts and humanities
- an integrated pattern of human knowledge, belief, and behavior that depends upon the capacity for symbolic thought and social learning
- the set of shared attitudes, values, goals, and practices that characterizes an institution, organization or group.

When the concept first emerged in eighteenth- and nineteenth-century Europe, it connoted a process of cultivation or improvement, as in agriculture or horticulture. In the nineteenth century, it came to refer first to the betterment or refinement of the individual, especially through education, and then to the fulfillment of national aspirations or ideals.

a. AStore
b. African Americans
c. Albert Einstein
d. Culture

12. _________, a business term, is a measure of how products and services supplied by a company meet or surpass customer expectation. It is seen as a key performance indicator within business and is part of the four perspectives of a Balanced Scorecard.

In a competitive marketplace where businesses compete for customers, _________ is seen as a key differentiator and increasingly has become a key element of business strategy.

a. Customer base
b. Customer satisfaction
c. Supplier diversity
d. Psychological pricing

13. In advertising, a _________ is an advertisement or campaign that uses a more direct, forceful, and overt sales message. This approach works in opposition to a soft sell.

Theorists have examined the value of repetition for _________ versus soft sell messages to determine their relative efficacy.

a. GL-70
b. Comparative advertising
c. Rack card
d. Hard sell

14. _________ is an advertisement in which a particular product specifically mentions a competitor by name for the express purpose of showing why the competitor is inferior to the product naming it.

This should not be confused with parody advertisements, where a fictional product is being advertised for the purpose of poking fun at the particular advertisement, nor should it be confused with the use of a coined brand name for the purpose of comparing the product without actually naming an actual competitor. ('Wikipedia tastes better and is less filling than the Encyclopedia Galactica.')

In the 1980s, during what has been referred to as the cola wars, soft-drink manufacturer Pepsi ran a series of advertisements where people, caught on hidden camera, in a blind taste test, chose Pepsi over rival Coca-Cola.

a. Comparative advertising
b. GL-70
c. Heavy-up
d. Cost per conversion

15. _________ is a range of services providing assistance with technology products such as mobile phones, televisions, computers, or other electronic or mechanical goods. In general, _________ services attempt to help the user solve specific problems with a product--rather than providing training, customization, or other support services.

Most companies offer _________ for the products they sell, either freely available or for a fee.

a. Technical support
b. 6-3-5 Brainwriting
c. 180SearchAssistant
d. Power III

16. In economics, business, retail, and accounting, a _________ is the value of money that has been used up to produce something, and hence is not available for use anymore. In economics, a _________ is an alternative that is given up as a result of a decision. In business, the _________ may be one of acquisition, in which case the amount of money expended to acquire it is counted as _________.

a. Cost
b. Variable cost
c. Transaction cost
d. Fixed costs

17. _________ describes the situation when output from (or information about the result of) an event or phenomenon in the past will influence the same event/phenomenon in the present or future. When an event is part of a chain of cause-and-effect that forms a circuit or loop, then the event is said to 'feed back' into itself.

_________ is also a synonym for:

- _________ Signal; the information about the initial event that is the basis for subsequent modification of the event.
- _________ Loop; the causal path that leads from the initial generation of the _________ signal to the subsequent modification of the event.

_________ is a mechanism, process or signal that is looped back to control a system within itself. Such a loop is called a _________ loop.

a. 180SearchAssistant
b. Power III
c. 6-3-5 Brainwriting
d. Feedback

18. _________ LLP, based in Chicago, was once one of the 'Big Five' accounting firms among PricewaterhouseCoopers, Deloitte Touche Tohmatsu, Ernst ' Young and KPMG, providing auditing, tax, and consulting services to large corporations. In 2002, the firm voluntarily surrendered its licenses to practice as Certified Public Accountants in the United States after being found guilty of criminal charges relating to the firm's handling of the auditing of Enron, the energy corporation, resulting in the loss of 85,000 jobs. Although the verdict was subsequently overturned by the Supreme Court of the United States, it has not returned as a viable business.

a. ADTECH
b. ACNielsen
c. AMAX
d. Arthur Andersen

19. _________ is the process of approaching prospective customers or clients, typically via telephone, who were not expecting such an interaction. The word 'cold' is used because the person receiving the call is not expecting a call or has not specifically asked to be contacted by a sales person.

Within the United Kingdom, the Privacy and Electronic Communications (EC Directive) Regulations 2003 make it unlawful to transmit an automated recorded message for direct marketing purposes via a telephone, without prior consent of the subscriber.

a. Cold calling
b. Direct Marketing Associations
c. Power III
d. Database marketing

20. In mathematics, an _________, or central tendency of a data set refers to a measure of the 'middle' or 'expected' value of the data set. There are many different descriptive statistics that can be chosen as a measurement of the central tendency of the data items.

An _________ is a single value that is meant to typify a list of values.

a. AMAX
b. ADTECH
c. ACNielsen
d. Average

21. A _________ or chief executive is typically the highest-ranking corporate officer (executive) or administrator in charge of total management of a corporation, company, organization reporting to the board of directors. In internal communication and press releases, many companies capitalize the term and those of other high positions, even when they are not proper nouns.

In some European Union countries, there are two separate boards, one executive board for the day-to-day business and one supervisory board for control purposes (elected by the shareholders.)

a. Power III
b. Decision Analyst
c. Financial analyst
d. Chief executive officer

22. _________ refers to a range of skills, tools, and techniques utilized to accomplish specific tasks, projects and goals. This set encompass a wide scope of activities, and these include planning, setting goals, delegation, analysis of time spent, monitoring, organizing, scheduling, and prioritizing. Initially _________ referred to just business or work activities, but eventually the term broadened to include personal activities also.

a. Digital strategy
b. Business plan
c. Goal setting
d. Time management

23. _________ refer to a collection of facts usually collected as the result of experience, observation or experiment or a set of premises. This may consist of numbers, words particularly as measurements or observations of a set of variables. _________ are often viewed as a lowest level of abstraction from which information and knowledge are derived.
a. Data
b. Mean
c. Pearson product-moment correlation coefficient
d. Sample size

24. _________ in organizations and public policy is both the organizational process of creating and maintaining a plan; and the psychological process of thinking about the activities required to create a desired goal on some scale. As such, it is a fundamental property of intelligent behavior. This thought process is essential to the creation and refinement of a plan, or integration of it with other plans, that is, it combines forecasting of developments with the preparation of scenarios of how to react to them.
a. Power III
b. Planning
c. 180SearchAssistant
d. 6-3-5 Brainwriting

25. A _________ is a systematic approach to selling a product or service. A growing body of published literature approaches the _________ from the point of view of an engineering discipline

Reasons for having a well thought-out _________ include seller and buyer risk management, standardized customer interaction in sales, and scalable revenue generation.

a. Sales management
b. Lead generation
c. Request for proposal
d. Sales process

26. _________ is defined by the American _________ Association as the activity, set of institutions, and processes for creating, communicating, delivering, and exchanging offerings that have value for customers, clients, partners, and society at large. The term developed from the original meaning which referred literally to going to market, as in shopping, or going to a market to sell goods or services.

_________ practice tends to be seen as a creative industry, which includes advertising, distribution and selling.

a. Product naming
b. Customer acquisition management
c. Marketing
d. Marketing myopia

27. _________ refers to messages and related media used to communicate with a market. Those who practice advertising, branding, direct marketing, graphic design, marketing, packaging, promotion, publicity, sponsorship, public relations, sales, sales promotion and online marketing are termed marketing communicators, _________ managers, or more briefly as marcom managers.

a. Sales promotion
b. Merchandising
c. Merchandise
d. Marketing communication

28. _________ is a term commonly used to describe commerce transactions between businesses like the one between a manufacturer and a wholesaler or a wholesaler and a retailer i.e both the buyer and the seller are business entity.This is unlike business-to-consumers (B2C) which involve a business entity and end consumer, or business-to-government (B2G) which involve a business entity and government.

The volume of B2B transactions is much higher than the volume of B2C transactions. The primary reason for this is that in a typical supply chain there will be many B2B transactions involving subcomponent or raw materials, and only one B2C transaction, specifically sale of the finished product to the end customer.

a. Customer relationship management
b. Social marketing
c. Disruptive technology
d. Business-to-business

29. _________ describes activities of businesses serving end consumers with products and/or services.

An example of a B2C transaction would be a person buying a pair of shoes from a retailer. The transactions that led to the shoes being available for purchase, that is the purchase of the leather, laces, rubber, etc.

a. Corporate capabilities package
b. Business-to-consumer
c. Societal marketing
d. Demand generation

30. _________ is the activity that the selling organization undertakes to reduce customer account defections. The success of this activity is when the customer account places an additional order before a 12-month period has expired. Note that ideally these orders will need to contribute similar financial amounts to the previous 12 months.
a. First-mover advantage
b. Customer centricity
c. Customer base
d. Customer retention

31. A _________ is a company or individual that purchases goods or services with the intention of reselling them rather than consuming or using them. This is usually done for profit (but could be resold at a loss.) One example can be found in the industry of telecommunications, where companies buy excess amounts of transmission capacity or call time from other carriers and resell it to smaller carriers.
a. Jobbing house
b. Value-based pricing
c. Discontinuation
d. Reseller

32. _________ is a broad label that refers to any individuals or households that use goods and services generated within the economy. The concept of a _________ is used in different contexts, so that the usage and significance of the term may vary.

A _________ is a person who uses any product or service.

a. 180SearchAssistant
b. 6-3-5 Brainwriting
c. Power III
d. Consumer

33. _________ is the physical search for minerals, fossils, precious metals or mineral specimens, and is also known as fossicking.

_________ is synonymous in some ways with mineral exploration which is an organised, large scale and at least semi-scientific effort undertaken by mineral resource companies to find commercially viable ore deposits. To actually be considered a prospector you must become registered as a professional prospector.

a. Prospecting
b. 180SearchAssistant
c. Power III
d. 6-3-5 Brainwriting

34. _________ is a method of direct marketing in which a salesperson solicits to prospective customers to buy products or services, either over the phone or through a subsequent face to face or Web conferencing appointment scheduled during the call.

_________ can also include recorded sales pitches programmed to be played over the phone via automatic dialing. _________ has come under fire in recent years, being viewed as an annoyance by many.

a. Phishing
b. Directory Harvest Attack
c. Joe job
d. Telemarketing

35. A _________ is a type of business entity in which partners (owners) share with each other the profits or losses of the business undertaking in which all have invested. _________s are often favored over corporations for taxation purposes, as the _________ structure does not generally incur a tax on profits before it is distributed to the partners (i.e. there is no dividend tax levied.) However, depending on the _________ structure and the jurisdiction in which it operates, owners of a _________ may be exposed to greater personal liability than they would as shareholders of a corporation.

a. Partnership
b. Fair Debt Collection Practices Act
c. Brand piracy
d. Competition law

36. A _________, in marketing, procurement, and organizational studies, is a group of employees, family members, or members of any type of organization responsible for purchasing an item for the organization. In a business setting, major purchases typically require input from various parts of the organization, including finance, accounting, purchasing, information technology management, and senior management. Highly technical purchases, such as information systems or production equipment, also require the expertise of technical specialists.

a. Marketing myopia
b. Commercialization
c. Packshot
d. Buying center

37. _________ is a sales technique in which a salesperson walks from one door of a house to another trying to sell a product or service to the general public. A variant of this involves cold calling first, when another sales representative attempts to gain agreement that a salesperson should visit. _________ selling is usually conducted in the afternoon hours, when the majority of people are at home.
a. Performance-based advertising
b. Fast moving consumer goods
c. Marketing management
d. Door-to-door

38. _________ refers to a business or organization attempting to acquire goods or services to accomplish the goals of the enterprise. Though there are several organizations that attempt to set standards in the _________ process, processes can vary greatly between organizations. Typically the word '_________' is not used interchangeably with the word 'procurement', since procurement typically includes Expediting, Supplier Quality, and Traffic and Logistics (T'L) in addition to _________.
a. Purchasing
b. Drop shipping
c. Supply network
d. Supply chain

39. _________ is the subjective judgment that people make about the characteristics and severity of a risk. The phrase is most commonly used in reference to natural hazards and threats to the environment or health, such as nuclear power. Several theories have been proposed to explain why different people make different estimates of the dangerousness of risks.
a. 6-3-5 Brainwriting
b. 180SearchAssistant
c. Power III
d. Risk perception

40. _________ is a concept that denotes the precise probability of specific eventualities. Technically, the notion of _________ is independent from the notion of value and, as such, eventualities may have both beneficial and adverse consequences. However, in general usage the convention is to focus only on potential negative impact to some characteristic of value that may arise from a future event.

a. 180SearchAssistant
b. 6-3-5 Brainwriting
c. Power III
d. Risk

41. _________ is a term in economics, where demand for one good or service occurs as a result of demand for another. This may occur as the former is a part of production of the second. For example, demand for coal leads to _________ for mining, as coal must be mined for coal to be consumed.
a. 6-3-5 Brainwriting
b. Power III
c. Derived demand
d. 180SearchAssistant

42. In economics, _________ is the desire to own something and the ability to pay for it. The term _________ signifies the ability or the willingness to buy a particular commodity at a given point of time .

.

a. Discretionary spending
b. Market dominance
c. Market system
d. Demand

43. A _________ is a retail establishment which specializes in selling a wide range of products without a single predominant merchandise line. _________s usually sell products including apparel, furniture, appliances, electronics, and additionally select other lines of products such as paint, hardware, toiletries, cosmetics, photographic equipment, jewelery, toys, and sporting goods. Certain _________s are further classified as discount _________s.
a. Power III
b. 6-3-5 Brainwriting
c. Department Store
d. 180SearchAssistant

44. Procter is a surname, and may also refer to:

- Bryan Waller Procter (pseud. Barry Cornwall), English poet
- Goodwin Procter, American law firm
- _________, consumer products multinational

.

a. Black PRies
b. Flyer
c. Convergent
d. Procter ' Gamble

1. _________, also referred to as i-marketing, web marketing, online marketing is the marketing of products or services over the Internet.

The Internet has brought many unique benefits to marketing, one of which being lower costs for the distribution of information and media to a global audience. The interactive nature of _________, both in terms of providing instant response and eliciting responses, is a unique quality of the medium.

a. Internet marketing
b. AMAX
c. ADTECH
d. ACNielsen

2. _________ is defined by the American _________ Association as the activity, set of institutions, and processes for creating, communicating, delivering, and exchanging offerings that have value for customers, clients, partners, and society at large. The term developed from the original meaning which referred literally to going to market, as in shopping, or going to a market to sell goods or services.

_________ practice tends to be seen as a creative industry, which includes advertising, distribution and selling.

a. Product naming
b. Marketing myopia
c. Marketing
d. Customer acquisition management

3. _________ is the difference between the revenues earned from and the costs associated with the customer relationship in a specified period.

According to Philip Kotler,'a profitable customer is a person, household or a company that overtime, yields a revenue stream that exceeds by an acceptable amount the company's cost stream of attracting, selling and servicing the customer'

Although _________ is nothing more than the result of applying the business concept of profit to a customer relationship, measuring the profitability of a firm's customers or customer groups can often deliver useful business insights.

Quite often a very small percentage of the firm's best customers will account for a large portion of firm profit.

a. Power III
b. Customer profitability
c. Cost management
d. 180SearchAssistant

4. The _________ is generally accepted as the use and specification of the four p's describing the strategic position of a product in the marketplace. One version of the origins of the _________ starts in 1948 when James Culliton said that a marketing decision should be a result of something similar to a recipe. This version continued in 1953 when Neil Borden, in his American Marketing Association presidential address, took the recipe idea one step further and coined the term 'Marketing-Mix'.

a. Power III
b. Marketing mix
c. 6-3-5 Brainwriting
d. 180SearchAssistant

5. _________ is difficult to define. For example, in 1952, Alfred Kroeber and Clyde Kluckhohn compiled a list of 164 definitions of '_________' in _________: A Critical Review of Concepts and Definitions. However, the word '_________' is most commonly used in three basic senses:

- excellence of taste in the fine arts and humanities
- an integrated pattern of human knowledge, belief, and behavior that depends upon the capacity for symbolic thought and social learning
- the set of shared attitudes, values, goals, and practices that characterizes an institution, organization or group.

When the concept first emerged in eighteenth- and nineteenth-century Europe, it connoted a process of cultivation or improvement, as in agriculture or horticulture. In the nineteenth century, it came to refer first to the betterment or refinement of the individual, especially through education, and then to the fulfillment of national aspirations or ideals.

a. African Americans
b. Culture
c. AStore
d. Albert Einstein

6. _________ refers to messages and related media used to communicate with a market. Those who practice advertising, branding, direct marketing, graphic design, marketing, packaging, promotion, publicity, sponsorship, public relations, sales, sales promotion and online marketing are termed marketing communicators, _________ managers, or more briefly as marcom managers.

a. Merchandising
b. Sales promotion
c. Merchandise
d. Marketing communication

7. _________ is a market coverage strategy in which a firm decides to ignore market segment differences and go after the whole market with one offer.it is type of marketing (or attempting to sell through persuasion) of a product to a wide audience. The idea is to broadcast a message that will reach the largest number of people possible. Traditionally _________ has focused on radio, television and newspapers as the medium used to reach this broad audience.
a. Cyberdoc
b. Marketspace
c. Mass marketing
d. Business-to-consumer

8. _________ refers to marketing strategies applied directly to a specific consumer.

Having the knowledge on the consumer preferences, there are suggested personalized products and promotions to each consumer.

The _________ is based in four main steps in order to fulfill its goals: Those stages are identify, differentiate, interact, and customize.

a. ADTECH
b. ACNielsen
c. AMAX
d. One-to-one marketing

9. _________ refers to the aggregated strategies of single business firm or a strategic business unit (SBU) in a diversified corporation. According to Michael Porter, a firm must formulate a _________ that incorporates either cost leadership, differentiation or focus in order to achieve a sustainable competitive advantage and long-term success in its chosen arenas or industries.

Functional strategies include marketing strategies, new product development strategies, human resource strategies, financial strategies, legal strategies, supply-chain strategies, and information technology management strategies.

a. Switching cost
b. Business strategy
c. Strategic business unit
d. Corporate strategy

10. A _________ is a type of business entity in which partners (owners) share with each other the profits or losses of the business undertaking in which all have invested. _________s are often favored over corporations for taxation purposes, as the _________ structure does not generally incur a tax on profits before it is distributed to the partners (i.e. there is no dividend tax levied.) However, depending on the _________ structure and the jurisdiction in which it operates, owners of a _________ may be exposed to greater personal liability than they would as shareholders of a corporation.
a. Partnership
b. Brand piracy
c. Competition law
d. Fair Debt Collection Practices Act

11. A _________ is a plan of action designed to achieve a particular goal.

_________ is different from tactics. In military terms, tactics is concerned with the conduct of an engagement while _________ is concerned with how different engagements are linked.

a. Power III
b. 6-3-5 Brainwriting
c. 180SearchAssistant
d. Strategy

12. The loyalty business model is a business model used in strategic management in which company resources are employed so as to increase the loyalty of customers and other stakeholders in the expectation that corporate objectives will be met or surpassed. A typical example of this type of model is: quality of product or service leads to customer satisfaction, which leads to _________, which leads to profitability.

Fredrick Reichheld (1996) expanded the loyalty business model beyond customers and employees.

a. Customer loyalty
b. 6-3-5 Brainwriting
c. 180SearchAssistant
d. Power III

13. _________ is the activity that the selling organization undertakes to reduce customer account defections. The success of this activity is when the customer account places an additional order before a 12-month period has expired. Note that ideally these orders will need to contribute similar financial amounts to the previous 12 months.

a. Customer centricity
b. Customer base
c. First-mover advantage
d. Customer retention

14. _________ is a term used to denote a section of the media specifically designed to reach a very large audience such as the population of a nation state. It was coined in the 1920s with the advent of nationwide radio networks, mass-circulation newspapers and magazines, although _________ were present centuries before the term became common. The term public media has a similar meaning: it is the sum of the public mass distributors of news and entertainment across media such as newspapers, television, radio, broadcasting, which may require union membership in some large markets such as Newspaper Guild, AFTRA, ' text publishers.

a. 6-3-5 Brainwriting
b. 180SearchAssistant
c. Power III
d. Mass media

15. A personal and cultural _________ is a relative ethic _________, an assumption upon which implementation can be extrapolated. A _________ system is a set of consistent _________s and measures that is soo not true. A principle _________ is a foundation upon which other _________s and measures of integrity are based.

a. Perceptual maps
b. Supreme Court of the United States
c. Package-on-Package
d. Value

16. _________ refer to a collection of facts usually collected as the result of experience, observation or experiment or a set of premises. This may consist of numbers, words particularly as measurements or observations of a set of variables. _________ are often viewed as a lowest level of abstraction from which information and knowledge are derived.

a. Pearson product-moment correlation coefficient
b. Sample size
c. Mean
d. Data

17. _________ is the process of extracting hidden patterns from data. As more data is gathered, with the amount of data doubling every three years, _________ is becoming an increasingly important tool to transform this data into information. It is commonly used in a wide range of profiling practices, such as marketing, surveillance, fraud detection and scientific discovery.

a. 180SearchAssistant
b. Structure mining
c. Data mining
d. Power III

18. In marketing, customer _________, lifetime customer value (LCV), or _________ (LTV) and a new concept of 'customer life cycle management' is the present value of the future cash flows attributed to the customer relationship. Use of customer _________ as a marketing metric tends to place greater emphasis on customer service and long-term customer satisfaction, rather than on maximizing short-term sales.

Customer _________ has intuitive appeal as a marketing concept, because in theory it represents exactly how much each customer is worth in monetary terms, and therefore exactly how much a marketing department should be willing to spend to acquire each customer.

a. Sweepstakes
b. Brand infiltration
c. Value chain
d. Lifetime value

19. In statistics, an _________ is a term in a statistical model added when the effect of two or more variables is not simply additive. Such a term reflects that the effect of one variable depends on the values of one or more other variables.

Thus, for a response Y and two variables x_1 and x_2 an additive model would be:

$$Y = ax_1 + bx_2 + \mathrm{error}$$

In contrast to this,

$$Y = ax_1 + bx_2 + c(x_1 \times x_2) + \mathrm{error},$$

is an example of a model with an _________ between variables x_1 and x_2 ('error' refers to the random variable whose value by which y differs from the expected value of y.)

a. AMAX
b. ADTECH
c. ACNielsen
d. Interaction

20. _________ in organizations and public policy is both the organizational process of creating and maintaining a plan; and the psychological process of thinking about the activities required to create a desired goal on some scale. As such, it is a fundamental property of intelligent behavior. This thought process is essential to the creation and refinement of a plan, or integration of it with other plans, that is, it combines forecasting of developments with the preparation of scenarios of how to react to them.
a. Power III
b. 6-3-5 Brainwriting
c. Planning
d. 180SearchAssistant

21. A _________ is a commercial building for storage of goods. _________s are used by manufacturers, importers, exporters, wholesalers, transport businesses, customs, etc. They are usually large plain buildings in industrial areas of cities and towns.
a. 180SearchAssistant
b. 6-3-5 Brainwriting
c. Warehouse
d. Power III

22. _________ can be regarded as an outcome of mental processes (cognitive process) leading to the selection of a course of action among several alternatives. Every _________ process produces a final choice. The output can be an action or an opinion of choice.
a. 180SearchAssistant
b. Power III
c. Decision making
d. 6-3-5 Brainwriting

23. _________ describes the situation when output from (or information about the result of) an event or phenomenon in the past will influence the same event/phenomenon in the present or future. When an event is part of a chain of cause-and-effect that forms a circuit or loop, then the event is said to 'feed back' into itself.

_________ is also a synonym for:

- _________ Signal; the information about the initial event that is the basis for subsequent modification of the event.
- _________ Loop; the causal path that leads from the initial generation of the _________ signal to the subsequent modification of the event.

_________ is a mechanism, process or signal that is looped back to control a system within itself. Such a loop is called a _________ loop.

a. 180SearchAssistant
b. Power III
c. Feedback
d. 6-3-5 Brainwriting

24. _________ is a broad label that refers to any individuals or households that use goods and services generated within the economy. The concept of a _________ is used in different contexts, so that the usage and significance of the term may vary.

A _________ is a person who uses any product or service.

a. 6-3-5 Brainwriting
b. Power III
c. 180SearchAssistant
d. Consumer

25. The _________ is a concept from business management that was first described and popularized by Michael Porter in his 1985 best-seller, Competitive Advantage: Creating and Sustaining Superior Performance.

A _________ is a chain of activities. Products pass through all activities of the chain in order and at each activity the product gains some value.

a. Value chain
b. Mass marketing
c. Business-to-business
d. Relationship management

26. A _________ is a brief statement of the purpose of a company, organization. It is ideally used to guide the actions of the organization.

_________s often contain the following:

- Purpose of the organization
- The organization's primary stakeholders: clients, stockholders, etc.
- Responsibilities of the organization towards these stockholders
- Products and services offered

Generally shorter _________s are more effective than longer ones.

In developing a _________:

- Encourage input as feasible from employees, volunteers, and other stakeholders
- Publicize it broadly

The _________ can be used to resolve differences between business stakeholders. Stakeholders include: employees including managers and executives, stockholders, board of directors, customers, suppliers, distributors, creditors, governments (local, state, federal, etc.), unions, competitors, NGO's, and the general public.

a. Power III
b. 180SearchAssistant
c. Mission statement
d. 6-3-5 Brainwriting

27. _________ is a measure of the strength of a brand, product, service relative to competitive offerings. There is often a geographic element to the competitive landscape. In defining _________, you must see to what extent a product, brand, or firm controls a product category in a given geographic area.

a. Market dominance
b. Market system
c. Productivity
d. Discretionary spending

28. Procter is a surname, and may also refer to:

- Bryan Waller Procter (pseud. Barry Cornwall), English poet
- Goodwin Procter, American law firm
- _________, consumer products multinational

.

a. Flyer
b. Procter ' Gamble
c. Convergent
d. Black PRies

29. _________ is understood as a business unit within the overall corporate identity which is distinguishable from other business because it serves a defined external market where management can conduct strategic planning in relation to products and markets. When companies become really large, they are best thought of as being composed of a number of businesses (or _________s.)

In the broader domain of strategic management, the phrase '_________' came into use in the 1960s, largely as a result of General Electric's many units.

a. Strategic business unit
b. Corporate strategy
c. Cost leadership
d. Business strategy

30.

Competitive advantage is, in very basic words, a position a firm occupies against its competitors. According to Michael Porter, the three methods for creating a _________ are through:

Cost leadership - Cost advantage occurs when a firm delivers the same services as its competitors but at a lower cost;

Differentiation - Differentiation advantage occurs when a firm delivers greater services for the same price of its competitors. They are collectively known as positional advantages because they denote the firm's position in its industry as a leader in either superior services or cost;

Focus (economics) - A focused approach requires the firm to concentrate on a narrow, exclusive competitive segment (market niche), hoping to achieve a local rather than industry wide competitive advantage. There are cost focus seekers, who aim to obtain a local cost advantage over competition and differentiation focuser, who are looking for a local difference.

a. Power III
b. 180SearchAssistant
c. Sustainable competitive advantage
d. 6-3-5 Brainwriting

31. Competitiveness is a comparative concept of the ability and performance of a firm, sub-sector or country to sell and supply goods and/or services in a given market. Although widely used in economics and business management, the usefulness of the concept, particularly in the context of national competitiveness, is vigorously disputed by economists, such as Paul Krugman .

The term may also be applied to markets, where it is used to refer to the extent to which the market structure may be regarded as perfectly _________.

a. Geographical pricing
b. Competitive
c. Free trade zone
d. Customs union

32. _________ is, in very basic words, a position a firm occupies against its competitors.

According to Michael Porter, the three methods for creating a sustainable _________ are through:

1. Cost leadership - Cost advantage occurs when a firm delivers the same services as its competitors but at a lower cost;

2.

a. 6-3-5 Brainwriting
b. 180SearchAssistant
c. Power III
d. Competitive advantage

33. In economics, business, retail, and accounting, a _________ is the value of money that has been used up to produce something, and hence is not available for use anymore. In economics, a _________ is an alternative that is given up as a result of a decision. In business, the _________ may be one of acquisition, in which case the amount of money expended to acquire it is counted as _________.

a. Transaction cost
b. Fixed costs
c. Variable cost
d. Cost

34. A supply chain is the system of organizations, people, technology, activities, information and resources involved in moving a product or service from _________ to customer. Supply chain activities transform natural resources, raw materials and components into a finished product that is delivered to the end customer. In sophisticated supply chain systems, used products may re-enter the supply chain at any point where residual value is recyclable.
a. Product line extension
b. Bringin' Home the Oil
c. Rebate
d. Supplier

35. A _________ is a process that can allow an organization to concentrate its limited resources on the greatest opportunities to increase sales and achieve a sustainable competitive advantage. A _________ should be centered around the key concept that customer satisfaction is the main goal.

A _________ is most effective when it is an integral component of corporate strategy, defining how the organization will successfully engage customers, prospects, and competitors in the market arena.

a. Cyberdoc
b. Marketing strategy
c. Psychographic
d. Societal marketing

36. _________ is a form of communication that typically attempts to persuade potential customers to purchase or to consume more of a particular brand of product or service. 'While now central to the contemporary global economy and the reproduction of global production networks, it is only quite recently that _________ has been more than a marginal influence on patterns of sales and production. The formation of modern _________ was intimately bound up with the emergence of new forms of monopoly capitalism around the end of the 19th and beginning of the 20th century as one element in corporate strategies to create, organize and where possible control markets, especially for mass produced consumer goods.
a. AMAX
b. ADTECH
c. ACNielsen
d. Advertising

37. The general definition of an _________ is an evaluation of a person, organization, system, process, project or product. _________s are performed to ascertain the validity and reliability of information; also to provide an assessment of a system's internal control. The goal of an _________ is to express an opinion on the person/organization/system (etc) in question, under evaluation based on work done on a test basis.

a. ADTECH
b. ACNielsen
c. Audit
d. AMAX

38. In economic models, the _________ time frame assumes no fixed factors of production. Firms can enter or leave the marketplace, and the cost (and availability) of land, labor, raw materials, and capital goods can be assumed to vary. In contrast, in the short-run time frame, certain factors are assumed to be fixed, because there is not sufficient time for them to change.

a. Power III
b. Long-run
c. 180SearchAssistant
d. 6-3-5 Brainwriting

39. _________ operations or facilities are commonly called 'distribution centers'. '_________' is the term generally used to describe the process or the work flow associated with the picking, packing and delivery of the packed item(s) to a shipping carrier.

a. ADTECH
b. AMAX
c. ACNielsen
d. Order processing

40. _________ is the practice of individuals including commercial businesses, governments and institutions, facilitating the sale of their products or services to other companies or organizations that in turn resell them, use them as components in products or services they offer _________ is also called business-to-_________ for short. (Note that while marketing to government entities shares some of the same dynamics of organizational marketing, B2G Marketing is meaningfully different.)

a. Business marketing
b. Law of disruption
c. Disruptive technology
d. Mass marketing

41. _________ is defined by the Oxford English Dictionary as 'the action or practice of selling among or between established clients, markets, traders, etc.' or 'that of selling an additional product or service to an existing customer'. In practice businesses define _________ in many different ways. Elements that might influence the definition might include: the size of the business, the industry sector it operates within and the financial motivations of those required to define the term.

a. Yield management
b. Service provider
c. Freebie marketing
d. Cross-selling

42. _________ is a business management strategy aimed at embedding awareness of quality in all organizational processes. _________ has been widely used in manufacturing, education, call centers, government, and service industries, as well as NASA space and science programs.

When used together as a phrase, the three words in this expression have the following meanings:

- Total: Involving the entire organization, supply chain, and/or product life cycle
- Quality: With its usual definitions, with all its complexities
- Management: The system of managing with steps like Plan, Organize, Control, Lead, Staff, provisioning and organizing.

As defined by the International Organization for Standardization (ISO):

> '_________ is a management approach for an organization, centered on quality, based on the participation of all its members and aiming at long-term success through customer satisfaction, and benefits to all members of the organization and to society.' ISO 8402:1994

One major aim is to reduce variation from every process so that greater consistency of effort is obtained. (Royse, D., Thyer, B., Padgett D., ' Logan T., 2006)

In Japan, _________ comprises four process steps, namely:

1. Kaizen - Focuses on 'Continuous Process Improvement', to make processes visible, repeatable and measurable.
2. Atarimae Hinshitsu - The idea that 'things will work as they are supposed to' .
3. Kansei - Examining the way the user applies the product leads to improvement in the product itself.
4. Miryokuteki Hinshitsu - The idea that 'things should have an aesthetic quality' (for example, a pen will write in a way that is pleasing to the writer.)

_________ requires that the company maintain this quality standard in all aspects of its business. This requires ensuring that things are done right the first time and that defects and waste are eliminated from operations.

a. 180SearchAssistant
b. Total quality management
c. Power III
d. 6-3-5 Brainwriting

43. _________ , according to The American Marketing Association, is 'a planning process designed to assure that all brand contacts received by a customer or prospect for a product, service, or organization are relevant to that person and consistent over time.' (Marketing Power Dictionary)

_________ is a term used to describe a holistic approach to marketing. It aims to ensure consistency of message and the complementary use of media. The concept includes online and offline marketing channels.

a. Integrated marketing communications
b. ADTECH
c. AMAX
d. ACNielsen

44. Human beings are also considered to be _________ because they have the ability to change raw materials into valuable _________. The term Human _________ can also be defined as the skills, energies, talents, abilities and knowledge that are used for the production of goods or the rendering of services. While taking into account human beings as _________, the following things have to be kept in mind:

- The size of the population
- The capabilities of the individuals in that population

Many _________ cannot be consumed in their original form. They have to be processed in order to change them into more usable commodities.

a. Power III
b. 180SearchAssistant
c. 6-3-5 Brainwriting
d. Resources

45. _________ is a retailing concept in which the total range of products sold by a retailer is broken down into discrete groups of similar or related products; these groups are known as product categories. Examples of grocery categories may be: tinned fish, washing detergent, toothpastes, etc.Each category is then run like a 'mini business' (Business Unit) in its own right, with its own set of turnover and/or profitability targets and strategies. An important facet of _________ is the shift in relationship between retailer and supplier : instead of the traditional adversarial relationship, the relationship moves to one of collaboration, exchange of information and data and joint business building.The focus of all negotiations is centered around the effects of the turnover of the total category, not just the sales on the individual products therein.

a. Brochure
b. Societal marketing
c. Market segment
d. Category management

46. _________ is one of the four elements of marketing mix. An organization or set of organizations (go-betweens) involved in the process of making a product or service available for use or consumption by a consumer or business user.

The other three parts of the marketing mix are product, pricing, and promotion.

a. Distribution
b. Comparison-Shopping agent
c. Japan Advertising Photographers' Association
d. Better Living Through Chemistry

47. _________ is an inventory strategy implemented to improve the return on investment of a business by reducing in-process inventory and its associated carrying costs. In order to achieve JIT the process must have signals of what is going on elsewhere within the process. This means that the process is often driven by a series of signals, which can be Kanban , that tell production processes when to make the next part.

a. Promotion
b. Personalization
c. Just-in-time
d. Clutter

48. _________ is one of the four Ps of the marketing mix. The other three aspects are product, promotion, and place. It is also a key variable in microeconomic price allocation theory.

a. Price
b. Relationship based pricing
c. Pricing
d. Competitor indexing

49. The business terms _________ and pull originated in the logistic and supply chain management, but are also widely used in marketing.

A _________-pull-system in business describes the move of a product or information between two subjects. On markets the consumers usually 'pulls' the goods or information they demand for their needs, while the offerers or suppliers '_________es' them toward the consumers.

a. Manufacturers' representatives
b. Completely randomized designs
c. Gold Key Matching Service
d. Push

50. A _________ is a company or individual that purchases goods or services with the intention of reselling them rather than consuming or using them. This is usually done for profit (but could be resold at a loss.) One example can be found in the industry of telecommunications, where companies buy excess amounts of transmission capacity or call time from other carriers and resell it to smaller carriers.
a. Reseller
b. Jobbing house
c. Discontinuation
d. Value-based pricing

51. An _________ is a special-purpose computer system designed to perform one or a few dedicated functions, often with real-time computing constraints. It is usually embedded as part of a complete device including hardware and mechanical parts. In contrast, a general-purpose computer, such as a personal computer, can do many different tasks depending on programming.
a. ACNielsen
b. Embedded system
c. AMAX
d. ADTECH

52. _________, a business term, is a measure of how products and services supplied by a company meet or surpass customer expectation. It is seen as a key performance indicator within business and is part of the four perspectives of a Balanced Scorecard.

In a competitive marketplace where businesses compete for customers, _________ is seen as a key differentiator and increasingly has become a key element of business strategy.

a. Psychological pricing
b. Supplier diversity
c. Customer base
d. Customer satisfaction

53. A _________ or logistics network is the system of organizations, people, technology, activities, information and resources involved in moving a product or service from supplier to customer. _________ activities transform natural resources, raw materials and components into a finished product that is delivered to the end customer. In sophisticated _________ systems, used products may re-enter the _________ at any point where residual value is recyclable.

a. Demand chain management
b. Purchasing
c. Supply chain network
d. Supply chain

1. _________ is defined by the American _________ Association as the activity, set of institutions, and processes for creating, communicating, delivering, and exchanging offerings that have value for customers, clients, partners, and society at large. The term developed from the original meaning which referred literally to going to market, as in shopping, or going to a market to sell goods or services.

_________ practice tends to be seen as a creative industry, which includes advertising, distribution and selling.

a. Customer acquisition management
b. Product naming
c. Marketing myopia
d. Marketing

2. _________ is subcontracting a process, such as product design or manufacturing, to a third-party company. The decision to outsource is often made in the interest of lowering cost or making better use of time and energy costs, redirecting or conserving energy directed at the competencies of a particular business, or to make more efficient use of land, labor, capital, (information) technology and resources. _________ became part of the business lexicon during the 1980s.
a. Intangible assets
b. In-house
c. ACNielsen
d. Outsourcing

3. _________s is the social science that studies the production, distribution, and consumption of goods and services. The term _________s comes from the Ancient Greek oá¼°κονομÎ¯α from oá¼¶κος (oikos, 'house') + vÏŒμος (nomos, 'custom' or 'law'), hence 'rules of the house(hold)'. Current _________ models developed out of the broader field of political economy in the late 19th century, owing to a desire to use an empirical approach more akin to the physical sciences.
a. ACNielsen
b. ADTECH
c. Industrial organization
d. Economic

4. In economics and related disciplines, a _________ is a cost incurred in making an economic exchange. For example, most people, when buying or selling a stock, must pay a commission to their broker; that commission is a _________ of doing the stock deal. Or consider buying a banana from a store; to purchase the banana, your costs will be not only the price of the banana itself, but also the energy and effort it requires to find out which of the various banana products you prefer, where to get them and at what price, the cost of traveling from your house to the store and back, the time waiting in line, and the effort of the paying itself; the costs above and beyond the cost of the banana are the _________s.

a. Transaction cost
b. Variable cost
c. Fixed costs
d. Marginal cost

5. In economics, business, retail, and accounting, a _________ is the value of money that has been used up to produce something, and hence is not available for use anymore. In economics, a _________ is an alternative that is given up as a result of a decision. In business, the _________ may be one of acquisition, in which case the amount of money expended to acquire it is counted as _________.

a. Cost
b. Variable cost
c. Transaction cost
d. Fixed costs

6. _________ is the study of the Earth and its lands, features, inhabitants, and phenomena. A literal translation would be 'to describe or write about the Earth'. The first person to use the word '_________' was Eratosthenes .

a. Power III
b. 6-3-5 Brainwriting
c. Geography
d. 180SearchAssistant

7. Procter is a surname, and may also refer to:

- Bryan Waller Procter (pseud. Barry Cornwall), English poet
- Goodwin Procter, American law firm
- _________, consumer products multinational

.

a. Convergent
b. Procter ' Gamble
c. Black PRies
d. Flyer

8. A _________ is a subgroup of people or organizations sharing one or more characteristics that cause them to have similar product and/or service needs. A true _________ meets all of the following criteria: it is distinct from other segments (different segments have different needs), it is homogeneous within the segment (exhibits common needs); it responds similarly to a market stimulus, and it can be reached by a market intervention. The term is also used when consumers with identical product and/or service needs are divided up into groups so they can be charged different amounts.

a. Customer insight
b. Commercial planning
c. Market segment
d. Production orientation

9. _________ is a method of direct marketing in which a salesperson solicits to prospective customers to buy products or services, either over the phone or through a subsequent face to face or Web conferencing appointment scheduled during the call.

_________ can also include recorded sales pitches programmed to be played over the phone via automatic dialing. _________ has come under fire in recent years, being viewed as an annoyance by many.

a. Phishing
b. Joe job
c. Telemarketing
d. Directory Harvest Attack

10. _________ describes activities of businesses serving end consumers with products and/or services.

An example of a B2C transaction would be a person buying a pair of shoes from a retailer. The transactions that led to the shoes being available for purchase, that is the purchase of the leather, laces, rubber, etc.

a. Societal marketing
b. Business-to-consumer
c. Corporate capabilities package
d. Demand generation

11. In accounting, _________ has a very specific meaning. It is an outflow of cash or other valuable assets from a person or company to another person or company. This outflow of cash is generally one side of a trade for products or services that have equal or better current or future value to the buyer than to the seller.
a. ADTECH
b. ACNielsen
c. AMAX
d. Expense

12. _________ is a marketing practice where two companies cooperate with separate distribution channels, sometimes including profit sharing. It is frequently confused with Co-promotion.

Cross-marketing describes the practice where two individual entities companies exchange marketing channels for mutual benefit.

a. SWOT analysis
b. Co-marketing
c. Vertical market
d. Confusion marketing

13. An _________ is a special-purpose computer system designed to perform one or a few dedicated functions, often with real-time computing constraints. It is usually embedded as part of a complete device including hardware and mechanical parts. In contrast, a general-purpose computer, such as a personal computer, can do many different tasks depending on programming.

a. ACNielsen
b. Embedded system
c. AMAX
d. ADTECH

14. _________ refers to the additional value of a commodity over the cost of commodities used to produce it from the previous stage of production. An example is the price of gasoline at the pump over the price of the oil in it. In national accounts used in macroeconomics, it refers to the contribution of the factors of production, i.e., land, labor, and capital goods, to raising the value of a product and corresponds to the incomes received by the owners of these factors. The factors of production provide 'services' which raise the unit price of a product (X) relative to the cost per unit of intermediate goods used up in the production of X. _________ is shared between the factors of production (capital, labor, also human capital), giving rise to issues of distribution.

a. Consumer spending
b. Deregulation
c. Power III
d. Value added

15. A _________ is a company or individual that purchases goods or services with the intention of reselling them rather than consuming or using them. This is usually done for profit (but could be resold at a loss.) One example can be found in the industry of telecommunications, where companies buy excess amounts of transmission capacity or call time from other carriers and resell it to smaller carriers.

a. Value-based pricing
b. Discontinuation
c. Jobbing house
d. Reseller

16. A _________ is a list of the general tasks and responsibilities of a position. Typically, it also includes to whom the position reports, specifications such as the qualifications needed by the person in the job, salary range for the position, etc. A _________ is usually developed by conducting a job analysis, which includes examining the tasks and sequences of tasks necessary to perform the job.

a. 180SearchAssistant
b. Power III
c. 6-3-5 Brainwriting
d. Job description

17. _________ and converging technologies are terms used to cover various cutting-edge developments in the emergence and convergence of technology.

_________ are those which represent new and significant developments within a field; converging techologies represent previously distinct fields which are in some way moving towards stronger inter-connection and similar goals.

Over time, new methods and topics are developed and opened up.

a. Arcis Communications
b. Emerging technologies
c. Interstate Bakeries
d. International organization

18. _________ is an advertisement in which a particular product specifically mentions a competitor by name for the express purpose of showing why the competitor is inferior to the product naming it.

This should not be confused with parody advertisements, where a fictional product is being advertised for the purpose of poking fun at the particular advertisement, nor should it be confused with the use of a coined brand name for the purpose of comparing the product without actually naming an actual competitor. ('Wikipedia tastes better and is less filling than the Encyclopedia Galactica.')

In the 1980s, during what has been referred to as the cola wars, soft-drink manufacturer Pepsi ran a series of advertisements where people, caught on hidden camera, in a blind taste test, chose Pepsi over rival Coca-Cola.

a. Heavy-up
b. GL-70
c. Comparative advertising
d. Cost per conversion

1. _________ can be regarded as an outcome of mental processes (cognitive process) leading to the selection of a course of action among several alternatives. Every _________ process produces a final choice. The output can be an action or an opinion of choice.

a. 6-3-5 Brainwriting
b. 180SearchAssistant
c. Power III
d. Decision making

2. _________ in organizations and public policy is both the organizational process of creating and maintaining a plan; and the psychological process of thinking about the activities required to create a desired goal on some scale. As such, it is a fundamental property of intelligent behavior. This thought process is essential to the creation and refinement of a plan, or integration of it with other plans, that is, it combines forecasting of developments with the preparation of scenarios of how to react to them.

a. 6-3-5 Brainwriting
b. Planning
c. 180SearchAssistant
d. Power III

3. _________ is the process of estimation in unknown situations. Prediction is a similar, but more general term. Both can refer to estimation of time series, cross-sectional or longitudinal data.

a. Power III
b. Forecasting
c. 6-3-5 Brainwriting
d. 180SearchAssistant

4. In economics, _________ is the desire to own something and the ability to pay for it. The term _________ signifies the ability or the willingness to buy a particular commodity at a given point of time .

.

a. Discretionary spending
b. Market system
c. Market dominance
d. Demand

5. In statistics, _________ is a technique that can be applied to time series data, either to produce smoothed data for presentation, or to make forecasts. The time series data themselves are a sequence of observations. The observed phenomenon may be an essentially random process, or it may be an orderly, but noisy, process.

a. ADTECH
b. AMAX
c. ACNielsen
d. Exponential smoothing

6. In statistics, a _________ rolling mean or running average, is a type of finite impulse response filter used to analyze a set of data points by creating a series of averages of different subsets of the full data set. A _________ is not a single number, but it is a set of numbers, each of which is the average of the corresponding subset of a larger set of data points. A _________ may also use unequal weights for each data value in the subset to emphasize particular values in the subset.
a. Confounding variables
b. Moving average
c. Frequency distribution
d. Statistics

7. In mathematics, an _________, or central tendency of a data set refers to a measure of the 'middle' or 'expected' value of the data set. There are many different descriptive statistics that can be chosen as a measurement of the central tendency of the data items.

An _________ is a single value that is meant to typify a list of values.

a. AMAX
b. ADTECH
c. ACNielsen
d. Average

8. In statistics and image processing, to smooth a data set is to create an approximating function that attempts to capture important patterns in the data, while leaving out noise or other fine-scale structures/rapid phenomena. Many different algorithms are used in _________. One of the most common algorithms is the 'moving average', often used to try to capture important trends in repeated statistical surveys.
a. 6-3-5 Brainwriting
b. Power III
c. 180SearchAssistant
d. Smoothing

9. _________ refers to the process by which tissues of dead organisms break down into simpler forms of matter. Such a breakdown of dead organisms is essential for new growth and development of living organisms because it recycles the finite chemical constituents and frees up the limited physical space in the biome. Bodies of living organisms begin to decompose shortly after death.

a. Decomposition
b. 6-3-5 Brainwriting
c. Power III
d. 180SearchAssistant

10. _________ is understood as a business unit within the overall corporate identity which is distinguishable from other business because it serves a defined external market where management can conduct strategic planning in relation to products and markets. When companies become really large, they are best thought of as being composed of a number of businesses (or _________s.)

In the broader domain of strategic management, the phrase '_________' came into use in the 1960s, largely as a result of General Electric's many units.

a. Cost leadership
b. Corporate strategy
c. Strategic business unit
d. Business strategy

11. An _________ is the manufacturing of a good or service within a category. Although _________ is a broad term for any kind of economic production, in economics and urban planning _________ is a synonym for the secondary sector, which is a type of economic activity involved in the manufacturing of raw materials into goods and products.

There are four key industrial economic sectors: the primary sector, largely raw material extraction industries such as mining and farming; the secondary sector, involving refining, construction, and manufacturing; the tertiary sector, which deals with services (such as law and medicine) and distribution of manufactured goods; and the quaternary sector, a relatively new type of knowledge _________ focusing on technological research, design and development such as computer programming, and biochemistry.

a. ADTECH
b. AMAX
c. ACNielsen
d. Industry

12. The _________ or _________ is used by business and government to classify and measure economic activity in Canada, Mexico and the United States. It has largely replaced the older Standard Industrial Classification system; however, certain government departments and agencies, such as the U.S. Securities and Exchange Commission (SEC), still use the SIC codes.

The _________ numbering system is a six-digit code.

a. Power III
b. 180SearchAssistant
c. 6-3-5 Brainwriting
d. North American Industry Classification System

13. _________ is a broad label that refers to any individuals or households that use goods and services generated within the economy. The concept of a _________ is used in different contexts, so that the usage and significance of the term may vary.

A _________ is a person who uses any product or service.

a. 6-3-5 Brainwriting
b. Power III
c. 180SearchAssistant
d. Consumer

14. _________ are final goods specifically intended for the mass market. For instance, _________ do not include investment assets, like precious antiques, even though these antiques are final goods.

Manufactured goods are goods that have been processed by way of machinery.

a. Durable good
b. Free good
c. Power III
d. Consumer goods

15. _________ is subcontracting a process, such as product design or manufacturing, to a third-party company. The decision to outsource is often made in the interest of lowering cost or making better use of time and energy costs, redirecting or conserving energy directed at the competencies of a particular business, or to make more efficient use of land, labor, capital, (information) technology and resources. _________ became part of the business lexicon during the 1980s.

a. In-house
b. ACNielsen
c. Intangible assets
d. Outsourcing

16. _________ is the study of the Earth and its lands, features, inhabitants, and phenomena. A literal translation would be 'to describe or write about the Earth'. The first person to use the word '_________' was Eratosthenes .

a. 6-3-5 Brainwriting
b. 180SearchAssistant
c. Power III
d. Geography

17. In the United States, the Office of Management and Budget (OMB) has produced a formal definition of metropolitan areas. These are referred to as '_________s' (_________s) and 'Combined Statistical Areas.' An earlier version of the _________ was the 'Standard _________' (SMetropolitan statistical area.) _________s are composed of counties and for some county equivalents.

a. 180SearchAssistant
b. Race and ethnicity in the United States Census
c. Metropolitan statistical area
d. Power III

18. _________ is systematic determination of merit, worth, and significance of something or someone using criteria against a set of standards. _________ often is used to characterize and appraise subjects of interest in a wide range of human enterprises, including the arts, criminal justice, foundations and non-profit organizations, government, health care, and other human services.

Depending on the topic of interest, there are professional groups which look to the quality and rigor of the _________ process.

a. Evaluation
b. AMAX
c. ADTECH
d. ACNielsen

19. In grammar, the _________ is the form of an adjective or adverb which denotes the degree or grade by which a person, thing and is used in this context with a subordinating conjunction, such as than, as...as, etc.

The structure of a _________ in English consists normally of the positive form of the adjective or adverb, plus the suffix -er e.g. 'he is taller than his father is', or 'the village is less picturesque than the town nearby'.

a. 6-3-5 Brainwriting
b. 180SearchAssistant
c. Comparative
d. Power III

20. _________ is the difference between the revenues earned from and the costs associated with the customer relationship in a specified period.

According to Philip Kotler,'a profitable customer is a person, household or a company that overtime, yields a revenue stream that exceeds by an acceptable amount the company's cost stream of attracting, selling and servicing the customer'

Although _________ is nothing more than the result of applying the business concept of profit to a customer relationship, measuring the profitability of a firm's customers or customer groups can often deliver useful business insights.

Quite often a very small percentage of the firm's best customers will account for a large portion of firm profit.

a. Cost management
b. Power III
c. 180SearchAssistant
d. Customer profitability

21. In accounting, _________ has a very specific meaning. It is an outflow of cash or other valuable assets from a person or company to another person or company. This outflow of cash is generally one side of a trade for products or services that have equal or better current or future value to the buyer than to the seller.
a. Expense
b. ACNielsen
c. AMAX
d. ADTECH

22. In statistics, _________ has two related meanings:

- the arithmetic _________
- the expected value of a random variable, which is also called the population _________.

It is sometimes stated that the '_________' _________s average. This is incorrect if '_________' is taken in the specific sense of 'arithmetic _________' as there are different types of averages: the _________, median, and mode. For instance, average house prices almost always use the median value for the average. These three types of averages are all measures of locations.

a. Confidence interval
b. Heteroskedastic
c. Standard normal distribution
d. Mean

23. The _________ or simply average deviation of a data set is the average of the absolute deviations and is a summary statistic of statistical dispersion or variability. It is also called the mean absolute deviation, but this is easily confused with the median absolute deviation.

The average absolute deviation of a set $\{x_1, x_2, ..., x_n\}$ is

$$\frac{1}{n}\sum_{i=1}^{n}|x_i - m(X)|$$

The choice of measure of central tendency, m(X), has a marked effect on the value of the average deviation.

a. ADTECH
b. ACNielsen
c. Average absolute deviation,
d. AMAX

24. _________s are errors in measurement that lead to measured values being inconsistent when repeated measures of a constant attribute or quantity are taken. The word random indicates that they are inherently unpredictable, and have null expected value, namely, they are scattered about the true value, and tend to have null arithmetic mean when a measurement is repeated several times with the same instrument. All measurements are prone to _________.
a. 180SearchAssistant
b. Power III
c. Systematic error
d. Random error

25. _________ is a term used by inventory specialists to describe a level of stock that is maintained below the cycle stock to buffer against stockouts. _________ exists to counter uncertainties in supply and demand. _________ is defined as extra units of inventory carried as protection against possible stockouts.
a. Cross-docking
b. Product support
c. Safety stock
d. Price-weighted

26. A _________ or logistics network is the system of organizations, people, technology, activities, information and resources involved in moving a product or service from supplier to customer. _________ activities transform natural resources, raw materials and components into a finished product that is delivered to the end customer. In sophisticated _________ systems, used products may re-enter the _________ at any point where residual value is recyclable.

a. Demand chain management
b. Purchasing
c. Supply chain network
d. Supply chain

1. _________ describes the situation when output from (or information about the result of) an event or phenomenon in the past will influence the same event/phenomenon in the present or future. When an event is part of a chain of cause-and-effect that forms a circuit or loop, then the event is said to 'feed back' into itself.

_________ is also a synonym for:

- _________ Signal; the information about the initial event that is the basis for subsequent modification of the event.
- _________ Loop; the causal path that leads from the initial generation of the _________ signal to the subsequent modification of the event.

_________ is a mechanism, process or signal that is looped back to control a system within itself. Such a loop is called a _________ loop.

a. Feedback
b. 6-3-5 Brainwriting
c. Power III
d. 180SearchAssistant

2. _________ is the process of estimation in unknown situations. Prediction is a similar, but more general term. Both can refer to estimation of time series, cross-sectional or longitudinal data.
a. 6-3-5 Brainwriting
b. Power III
c. 180SearchAssistant
d. Forecasting

3. _________ is the set of reasons that determines one to engage in a particular behavior. The term is generally used for human _________ but, theoretically, it can be used to describe the causes for animal behavior as well
a. Power III
b. 180SearchAssistant
c. Role playing
d. Motivation

4. Importance of _________ is critical for any commercial organization. Expanding business is not possible without increasing sales volumes, and effective _________ goal is to organize sales team work in such a manner that ensures a growing flow of regular customers and increasing amount of sales.

The four phase-model of Management Process

1. Conception
2. Planning
3. Execution
4. Control

This model is cyclical, so it is a constant/continuous process.

===_________ is attainment of sales force goals in a effective ' efficient manner through planning, staffing, training, leading ' controlling organizational resources.

a. Request for proposal
b. Hit rate
c. Sales management
d. Sales process

5. In algebra, a _________ is a function depending on n that associates a scalar, det(A), to an n×n square matrix A. The fundamental geometric meaning of a _________ is a scale factor for measure when A is regarded as a linear transformation. _________s are important both in calculus, where they enter the substitution rule for several variables, and in multilinear algebra.

For a fixed nonnegative integer n, there is a unique _________ function for the n×n matrices over any commutative ring R. In particular, this function exists when R is the field of real or complex numbers.

a. Motion Picture Association of America's film-rating system
b. Black Friday
c. Package-on-Package
d. Determinant

6. _________s are used in open sentences. For instance, in the formula x + 1 = 5, x is a _________ which represents an 'unknown' number. _________s are often represented by letters of the Roman alphabet, or those of other alphabets, such as Greek, and use other special symbols.

a. Variable
b. Quantitative
c. Book of business
d. Personalization

7. In psychology, philosophy, and the cognitive sciences, _________ is the process of attaining awareness or understanding of sensory information. It is a task far more complex than was imagined in the 1950s and 1960s, when it was predicted that building perceiving machines would take about a decade, a goal which is still very far from fruition. The word _________ comes from the Latin words _________, percepio, meaning 'receiving, collecting, action of taking possession, apprehension with the mind or senses.'

_________ is one of the oldest fields in psychology.

a. Groupthink
b. Power III
c. 180SearchAssistant
d. Perception

8. In economics and sociology, an _________ is any factor (financial or non-financial) that enables or motivates a particular course of action, or counts as a reason for preferring one choice to the alternatives. It is an expectation that encourages people to behave in a certain way. Since human beings are purposeful creatures, the study of _________ structures is central to the study of all economic activity (both in terms of individual decision-making and in terms of co-operation and competition within a larger institutional structure.)

a. ACNielsen
b. ADTECH
c. AMAX
d. Incentive

9. A _________ is the space, actual or metaphorical, in which a market operates. The term is also used in a trademark law context to denote the actual consumer environment, ie. the 'real world' in which products and services are provided and consumed.

a. Marketplace
b. 6-3-5 Brainwriting
c. 180SearchAssistant
d. Power III

10. In economics, business, retail, and accounting, a _________ is the value of money that has been used up to produce something, and hence is not available for use anymore. In economics, a _________ is an alternative that is given up as a result of a decision. In business, the _________ may be one of acquisition, in which case the amount of money expended to acquire it is counted as _________.

a. Cost
b. Variable cost
c. Transaction cost
d. Fixed costs

11. _________ involves disseminating information about a product, product line, brand, or company. It is one of the four key aspects of the marketing mix. (The other three elements are product marketing, pricing, and distribution). P>_________ is generally sub-divided into two parts:

- Above the line _________: Promotion in the media (e.g. TV, radio, newspapers, Internet and Mobile Phones) in which the advertiser pays an advertising agency to place the ad
- Below the line _________: All other _________. Much of this is intended to be subtle enough for the consumer to be unaware that _________ is taking place. E.g. sponsorship, product placement, endorsements, sales _________, merchandising, direct mail, personal selling, public relations, trade shows

a. Cashmere Agency
b. Davie Brown Index
c. Promotion
d. Bottling lines

12. _________ is a branch of philosophy which seeks to address questions about morality, such as how a moral outcome can be achieved in a specific situation (applied _________), how moral values should be determined (normative _________), what moral values people actually abide by (descriptive _________), what the fundamental semantic, ontological, and epistemic nature of _________ or morality is (meta-_________), and how moral capacity or moral agency develops and what its nature is (moral psychology.)

Socrates was one of the first Greek philosophers to encourage both scholars and the common citizen to turn their attention from the outside world to the condition of man. In this view, Knowledge having a bearing on human life was placed highest, all other knowledge being secondary.

a. AMAX
b. ACNielsen
c. ADTECH
d. Ethics

13. A _________ is a retail establishment which specializes in selling a wide range of products without a single predominant merchandise line. _________s usually sell products including apparel, furniture, appliances, electronics, and additionally select other lines of products such as paint, hardware, toiletries, cosmetics, photographic equipment, jewelery, toys, and sporting goods. Certain _________s are further classified as discount _________s.

a. 180SearchAssistant
b. 6-3-5 Brainwriting
c. Power III
d. Department Store

14. _________ is defined by the American _________ Association as the activity, set of institutions, and processes for creating, communicating, delivering, and exchanging offerings that have value for customers, clients, partners, and society at large. The term developed from the original meaning which referred literally to going to market, as in shopping, or going to a market to sell goods or services.

_________ practice tends to be seen as a creative industry, which includes advertising, distribution and selling.

a. Marketing
b. Marketing myopia
c. Product naming
d. Customer acquisition management

15. _________ refers to messages and related media used to communicate with a market. Those who practice advertising, branding, direct marketing, graphic design, marketing, packaging, promotion, publicity, sponsorship, public relations, sales, sales promotion and online marketing are termed marketing communicators, _________ managers, or more briefly as marcom managers.
a. Sales promotion
b. Merchandising
c. Merchandise
d. Marketing communication

16. In environmental modeling and especially in hydrology, a _________ model means a model that is acceptably consistent with observed natural processes, i.e. that simulates well, for example, observed river discharge. It is a key concept of the so-called Generalized Likelihood Uncertainty Estimation (GLUE) methodology to quantify how uncertain environmental predictions are.
a. Behavioral
b. Power III
c. 6-3-5 Brainwriting
d. 180SearchAssistant

1. _________ is the set of reasons that determines one to engage in a particular behavior. The term is generally used for human _________ but, theoretically, it can be used to describe the causes for animal behavior as well

a. Role playing
b. Power III
c. 180SearchAssistant
d. Motivation

2. In economics and sociology, an _________ is any factor (financial or non-financial) that enables or motivates a particular course of action, or counts as a reason for preferring one choice to the alternatives. It is an expectation that encourages people to behave in a certain way. Since human beings are purposeful creatures, the study of _________ structures is central to the study of all economic activity (both in terms of individual decision-making and in terms of co-operation and competition within a larger institutional structure.)

a. AMAX
b. ADTECH
c. ACNielsen
d. Incentive

3. In psychology, philosophy, and the cognitive sciences, _________ is the process of attaining awareness or understanding of sensory information. It is a task far more complex than was imagined in the 1950s and 1960s, when it was predicted that building perceiving machines would take about a decade, a goal which is still very far from fruition. The word _________ comes from the Latin words _________, percepio, meaning 'receiving, collecting, action of taking possession, apprehension with the mind or senses.'

_________ is one of the oldest fields in psychology.

a. 180SearchAssistant
b. Perception
c. Groupthink
d. Power III

4. _________ is defined by the American _________ Association as the activity, set of institutions, and processes for creating, communicating, delivering, and exchanging offerings that have value for customers, clients, partners, and society at large. The term developed from the original meaning which referred literally to going to market, as in shopping, or going to a market to sell goods or services.

_________ practice tends to be seen as a creative industry, which includes advertising, distribution and selling.

a. Product naming
b. Customer acquisition management
c. Marketing myopia
d. Marketing

5. _________ refers to messages and related media used to communicate with a market. Those who practice advertising, branding, direct marketing, graphic design, marketing, packaging, promotion, publicity, sponsorship, public relations, sales, sales promotion and online marketing are termed marketing communicators, _________ managers, or more briefly as marcom managers.
a. Sales promotion
b. Merchandise
c. Merchandising
d. Marketing communication

6. A _________ is the space, actual or metaphorical, in which a market operates. The term is also used in a trademark law context to denote the actual consumer environment, ie. the 'real world' in which products and services are provided and consumed.
a. 6-3-5 Brainwriting
b. 180SearchAssistant
c. Power III
d. Marketplace

7. _________s are used in open sentences. For instance, in the formula x + 1 = 5, x is a _________ which represents an 'unknown' number. _________s are often represented by letters of the Roman alphabet, or those of other alphabets, such as Greek, and use other special symbols.
a. Quantitative
b. Personalization
c. Book of business
d. Variable

8. _________ or _________ data refers to selected population characteristics as used in government, marketing or opinion research, or the _________ profiles used in such research. Note the distinction from the term 'demography' Commonly-used _________ include race, age, income, disabilities, mobility (in terms of travel time to work or number of vehicles available), educational attainment, home ownership, employment status, and even location.

a. African Americans
b. AStore
c. Albert Einstein
d. Demographic

9. In economics, _________ is a measure of the relative satisfaction from consumption of various goods and services. Given this measure, one may speak meaningfully of increasing or decreasing _________, and thereby explain economic behavior in terms of attempts to increase one's _________. For illustrative purposes, changes in _________ are sometimes expressed in units called utils.

a. AMAX
b. ACNielsen
c. Utility
d. ADTECH

10. In economics, an externality or spillover of an economic transaction is an impact on a party that is not directly involved in the transaction. In such a case, prices do not reflect the full costs or benefits in production or consumption of a product or service. A positive impact is called an _________ benefit, while a negative impact is called an _________ cost.

a. AMAX
b. External
c. ACNielsen
d. ADTECH

11. _________ is a term commonly used to describe commerce transactions between businesses like the one between a manufacturer and a wholesaler or a wholesaler and a retailer i.e both the buyer and the seller are business entity.This is unlike business-to-consumers (B2C) which involve a business entity and end consumer, or business-to-government (B2G) which involve a business entity and government.

The volume of B2B transactions is much higher than the volume of B2C transactions. The primary reason for this is that in a typical supply chain there will be many B2B transactions involving subcomponent or raw materials, and only one B2C transaction, specifically sale of the finished product to the end customer.

a. Disruptive technology
b. Customer relationship management
c. Social marketing
d. Business-to-business

1. A _________ is a type of wholesale merchant business that buys goods and bulk products from importers, other wholesalers and then sells to retailers. _________s can deal in any commodity destined for the retail market. Typical categories are food, lumber, hardware, fuel, and textiles.
   a. Chief privacy officer
   b. Refusal to deal
   c. Tacit collusion
   d. Jobbing house

2. An _________ is the manufacturing of a good or service within a category. Although _________ is a broad term for any kind of economic production, in economics and urban planning _________ is a synonym for the secondary sector, which is a type of economic activity involved in the manufacturing of raw materials into goods and products.

There are four key industrial economic sectors: the primary sector, largely raw material extraction industries such as mining and farming; the secondary sector, involving refining, construction, and manufacturing; the tertiary sector, which deals with services (such as law and medicine) and distribution of manufactured goods; and the quaternary sector, a relatively new type of knowledge _________ focusing on technological research, design and development such as computer programming, and biochemistry.

   a. ACNielsen
   b. ADTECH
   c. AMAX
   d. Industry

3. In psychology, philosophy, and the cognitive sciences, _________ is the process of attaining awareness or understanding of sensory information. It is a task far more complex than was imagined in the 1950s and 1960s, when it was predicted that building perceiving machines would take about a decade, a goal which is still very far from fruition. The word _________ comes from the Latin words _________, percepio, meaning 'receiving, collecting, action of taking possession, apprehension with the mind or senses.'

_________ is one of the oldest fields in psychology.

   a. Power III
   b. 180SearchAssistant
   c. Groupthink
   d. Perception

4. _________ is the set of reasons that determines one to engage in a particular behavior. The term is generally used for human _________ but, theoretically, it can be used to describe the causes for animal behavior as well

a. Power III
b. 180SearchAssistant
c. Role playing
d. Motivation

5. _________s are used in open sentences. For instance, in the formula x + 1 = 5, x is a _________ which represents an 'unknown' number. _________s are often represented by letters of the Roman alphabet, or those of other alphabets, such as Greek, and use other special symbols.
a. Personalization
b. Book of business
c. Quantitative
d. Variable

6. In algebra, a _________ is a function depending on n that associates a scalar, det(A), to an n×n square matrix A. The fundamental geometric meaning of a _________ is a scale factor for measure when A is regarded as a linear transformation. _________s are important both in calculus, where they enter the substitution rule for several variables, and in multilinear algebra.

For a fixed nonnegative integer n, there is a unique _________ function for the n×n matrices over any commutative ring R. In particular, this function exists when R is the field of real or complex numbers.

a. Package-on-Package
b. Determinant
c. Motion Picture Association of America's film-rating system
d. Black Friday

7. In economics, an externality or spillover of an economic transaction is an impact on a party that is not directly involved in the transaction. In such a case, prices do not reflect the full costs or benefits in production or consumption of a product or service. A positive impact is called an _________ benefit, while a negative impact is called an _________ cost.
a. ACNielsen
b. External
c. AMAX
d. ADTECH

8. In economics, business, retail, and accounting, a _________ is the value of money that has been used up to produce something, and hence is not available for use anymore. In economics, a _________ is an alternative that is given up as a result of a decision. In business, the _________ may be one of acquisition, in which case the amount of money expended to acquire it is counted as _________.

a. Transaction cost
b. Fixed costs
c. Cost
d. Variable cost

9. A _________ is the space, actual or metaphorical, in which a market operates. The term is also used in a trademark law context to denote the actual consumer environment, ie. the 'real world' in which products and services are provided and consumed.
a. Power III
b. 6-3-5 Brainwriting
c. Marketplace
d. 180SearchAssistant

10. _________ is a term commonly used to describe commerce transactions between businesses like the one between a manufacturer and a wholesaler or a wholesaler and a retailer i.e both the buyer and the seller are business entity.This is unlike business-to-consumers (B2C) which involve a business entity and end consumer, or business-to-government (B2G) which involve a business entity and government.

The volume of B2B transactions is much higher than the volume of B2C transactions. The primary reason for this is that in a typical supply chain there will be many B2B transactions involving subcomponent or raw materials, and only one B2C transaction, specifically sale of the finished product to the end customer.

a. Customer relationship management
b. Business-to-business
c. Social marketing
d. Disruptive technology

11. _________ or _________ data refers to selected population characteristics as used in government, marketing or opinion research, or the _________ profiles used in such research. Note the distinction from the term 'demography' Commonly-used _________ include race, age, income, disabilities, mobility (in terms of travel time to work or number of vehicles available), educational attainment, home ownership, employment status, and even location.
a. AStore
b. African Americans
c. Albert Einstein
d. Demographic

12. A _________ or digger group is a sociological group that does not constitute a politically dominant voting majority of the total population of a given society. A sociological _________ is not necessarily a numerical _________ -- it may include any group that is subnormal with respect to a dominant group in terms of social status, education, employment, wealth and political power. To avoid confusion, some writers prefer the terms 'subordinate group' and 'dominant group' rather than '_________' and 'majority', respectively.
   a. Reference group
   b. Minority
   c. Mociology
   d. Power III

13. _________ is a contract between two parties, one being the employer and the other being the employee. An employee may be defined as: 'A person in the service of another under any contract of hire, express or implied, oral or written, where the employer has the power or right to control and direct the employee in the material details of how the work is to be performed.' Black's Law Dictionary page 471 (5th ed. 1979.)
   a. AMAX
   b. ADTECH
   c. ACNielsen
   d. Employment

14. In economics and sociology, an _________ is any factor (financial or non-financial) that enables or motivates a particular course of action, or counts as a reason for preferring one choice to the alternatives. It is an expectation that encourages people to behave in a certain way. Since human beings are purposeful creatures, the study of _________ structures is central to the study of all economic activity (both in terms of individual decision-making and in terms of co-operation and competition within a larger institutional structure.)
   a. ACNielsen
   b. ADTECH
   c. Incentive
   d. AMAX

15. _________ is the variety of human societies or cultures in a specific region, or in the world as a whole. (The term is also sometimes used to refer to multiculturalism within an organisation)
   a. 6-3-5 Brainwriting
   b. Cultural diversity
   c. 180SearchAssistant
   d. Power III

16. Procter is a surname, and may also refer to:

- Bryan Waller Procter (pseud. Barry Cornwall), English poet
- Goodwin Procter, American law firm
- _________, consumer products multinational

.

a. Black PRies
b. Flyer
c. Convergent
d. Procter ' Gamble

17. Cognition is the scientific term for 'the process of thought.' Its usage varies in different ways in accord with different disciplines: For example, in psychology and _________ science it refers to an information processing view of an individual's psychological functions. Other interpretations of the meaning of cognition link it to the development of concepts; individual minds, groups, organizations, and even larger coalitions of entities, can be modelled as 'societies' (Society of Mind), which cooperate to form concepts.

The autonomous elements of each 'society' would have the opportunity to demonstrate emergent behavior in the face of some crisis or opportunity.

a. 180SearchAssistant
b. Power III
c. 6-3-5 Brainwriting
d. Cognitive

18. _________ was originally coined by Austrian psychologist Alfred Adler in 1929. The current broader sense of the word dates from 1961.

In sociology, a _________ is the way a person lives.

a. Lifestyle
b. 180SearchAssistant
c. 6-3-5 Brainwriting
d. Power III

19. A _________ is defined by the International Co-operative Alliance's Statement on the Co-operative Identity as an autonomous association of persons united voluntarily to meet their common economic, social, and cultural needs and aspirations through a jointly-owned and democratically-controlled enterprise. It is a business organization owned and operated by a group of individuals for their mutual benefit. A _________ may also be defined as a business owned and controlled equally by the people who use its services or who work at it.

a. 6-3-5 Brainwriting
b. Cooperative
c. Power III
d. 180SearchAssistant

20. _________ describes activities of businesses serving end consumers with products and/or services.

An example of a B2C transaction would be a person buying a pair of shoes from a retailer. The transactions that led to the shoes being available for purchase, that is the purchase of the leather, laces, rubber, etc.

a. Demand generation
b. Corporate capabilities package
c. Societal marketing
d. Business-to-consumer

21. Importance of _________ is critical for any commercial organization. Expanding business is not possible without increasing sales volumes, and effective _________ goal is to organize sales team work in such a manner that ensures a growing flow of regular customers and increasing amount of sales.

The four phase-model of Management Process

1. Conception
2. Planning
3. Execution
4. Control

This model is cyclical, so it is a constant/continuous process.

===_________ is attainment of sales force goals in a effective ' efficient manner through planning, staffing, training, leading ' controlling organizational resources.

a. Sales process
b. Sales management
c. Hit rate
d. Request for proposal

1. In economics, an externality or spillover of an economic transaction is an impact on a party that is not directly involved in the transaction. In such a case, prices do not reflect the full costs or benefits in production or consumption of a product or service. A positive impact is called an _________ benefit, while a negative impact is called an _________ cost.

a. AMAX
b. ADTECH
c. ACNielsen
d. External

2. _________ is a contract between two parties, one being the employer and the other being the employee. An employee may be defined as: 'A person in the service of another under any contract of hire, express or implied, oral or written, where the employer has the power or right to control and direct the employee in the material details of how the work is to be performed.' Black's Law Dictionary page 471 (5th ed. 1979.)

a. Employment
b. ACNielsen
c. AMAX
d. ADTECH

3. _________s are used in open sentences. For instance, in the formula x + 1 = 5, x is a _________ which represents an 'unknown' number. _________s are often represented by letters of the Roman alphabet, or those of other alphabets, such as Greek, and use other special symbols.

a. Book of business
b. Quantitative
c. Personalization
d. Variable

4. _________ can be regarded as an outcome of mental processes (cognitive process) leading to the selection of a course of action among several alternatives. Every _________ process produces a final choice. The output can be an action or an opinion of choice.

a. 6-3-5 Brainwriting
b. Decision making
c. Power III
d. 180SearchAssistant

5. _________ in organizations and public policy is both the organizational process of creating and maintaining a plan; and the psychological process of thinking about the activities required to create a desired goal on some scale. As such, it is a fundamental property of intelligent behavior. This thought process is essential to the creation and refinement of a plan, or integration of it with other plans, that is, it combines forecasting of developments with the preparation of scenarios of how to react to them.

a. 6-3-5 Brainwriting
b. 180SearchAssistant
c. Power III
d. Planning

6. _________ refers to various methodologies for analyzing the requirements of a job.

The general purpose of _________ is to document the requirements of a job and the work performed. Job and task analysis is performed as a basis for later improvements, including: definition of a job domain; describing a job; developing performance appraisals, selection systems, promotion criteria, training needs assessment, and compensation plans.

a. Job analysis
b. Cross-functional team
c. Power III
d. 180SearchAssistant

7. A _________ is a list of the general tasks and responsibilities of a position. Typically, it also includes to whom the position reports, specifications such as the qualifications needed by the person in the job, salary range for the position, etc. A _________ is usually developed by conducting a job analysis, which includes examining the tasks and sequences of tasks necessary to perform the job.
a. Job description
b. 6-3-5 Brainwriting
c. Power III
d. 180SearchAssistant

8. A _________ is the space, actual or metaphorical, in which a market operates. The term is also used in a trademark law context to denote the actual consumer environment, ie. the 'real world' in which products and services are provided and consumed.
a. Marketplace
b. Power III
c. 180SearchAssistant
d. 6-3-5 Brainwriting

9. _________ is a form of communication that typically attempts to persuade potential customers to purchase or to consume more of a particular brand of product or service. 'While now central to the contemporary global economy and the reproduction of global production networks, it is only quite recently that _________ has been more than a marginal influence on patterns of sales and production. The formation of modern _________ was intimately bound up with the emergence of new forms of monopoly capitalism around the end of the 19th and beginning of the 20th century as one element in corporate strategies to create, organize and where possible control markets, especially for mass produced consumer goods.

a. Advertising
b. ACNielsen
c. AMAX
d. ADTECH

10. In economics, business, retail, and accounting, a _________ is the value of money that has been used up to produce something, and hence is not available for use anymore. In economics, a _________ is an alternative that is given up as a result of a decision. In business, the _________ may be one of acquisition, in which case the amount of money expended to acquire it is counted as _________.

a. Transaction cost
b. Fixed costs
c. Variable cost
d. Cost

11. _________ is a measure of the strength of a brand, product, service relative to competitive offerings. There is often a geographic element to the competitive landscape. In defining _________, you must see to what extent a product, brand, or firm controls a product category in a given geographic area.

a. Market dominance
b. Market system
c. Productivity
d. Discretionary spending

12. An _________ is a company that matches workers to open jobs. The first _________ in the United States was opened by Fred Winslow who opened Engineering Agency in 1893. It later became part of General Employment Enterprises who also owned Businessmen's Clearing House (est.

a. Employment agency
b. AMAX
c. ADTECH
d. ACNielsen

13. _________ is an employment website owned by Monster Worldwide. Monster is one of the 20 most visited websites out of 100 million worldwide, according to comScore Media Metrics (November 2006.) It was created in 1999 by the merger of The Monster Board (TMB) and Online Career Center (OCC), which were two of the first and most popular career web sites on the Internet.

a. Monster.com
b. Power III
c. 6-3-5 Brainwriting
d. 180SearchAssistant

14. The _________ of 1990 (ADA) is the short title of United States (Pub.L. 101-336, 104 Stat. 327, enacted July 26, 1990), codified at 42 U.S.C.Â§ 12101 et seq. It was signed into law on July 26, 1990, by President George H. W. Bush, and later amended with changes effective January 1, 2009. The _________ is a wide-ranging civil rights law that prohibits, under certain circumstances, discrimination based on disability. It affords similar protections against discrimination to Americans with disabilities as the Civil Rights Act of 1964,

a. AMAX
b. Americans with Disabilities Act
c. ACNielsen
d. ADTECH

15. _________ is a fee paid on borrowed assets. It is the price paid for the use of borrowed money , or, money earned by deposited funds . Assets that are sometimes lent with _________ include money, shares, consumer goods through hire purchase, major assets such as aircraft, and even entire factories in finance lease arrangements.

a. ACNielsen
b. ADTECH
c. AMAX
d. Interest

16. _________ is a list for goods and materials held available in stock by a business. It is also used for a list of the contents of a household and for a list for testamentary purposes of the possessions of someone who has died. In accounting _________ is considered an asset.

a. Inventory
b. Ending Inventory
c. ADTECH
d. ACNielsen

17. A _________ aims to describe aspects of a person's character that remain stable throughout that person's lifetime, the individual's character pattern of behavior, thoughts, and feelings. An early model of personality was posited by Greek philosopher/physician Hippocrates. The 20th century heralded a new interest in defining and identifying separate personality types, in close correlation with the emergence of the field of psychology.

a. Personality test
b. Power III
c. 6-3-5 Brainwriting
d. 180SearchAssistant

1. In economics, business, retail, and accounting, a _________ is the value of money that has been used up to produce something, and hence is not available for use anymore. In economics, a _________ is an alternative that is given up as a result of a decision. In business, the _________ may be one of acquisition, in which case the amount of money expended to acquire it is counted as _________.

a. Fixed costs
b. Variable cost
c. Transaction cost
d. Cost

2. _________ in economics refers to metrics and measures of output from production processes, per unit of input. Labor _________, for example, is typically measured as a ratio of output per labor-hour, an input. _________ may be conceived of as a metrics of the technical or engineering efficiency of production.

a. Power III
b. Productivity
c. Value engineering
d. 180SearchAssistant

3. An _________ is the manufacturing of a good or service within a category. Although _________ is a broad term for any kind of economic production, in economics and urban planning _________ is a synonym for the secondary sector, which is a type of economic activity involved in the manufacturing of raw materials into goods and products.

There are four key industrial economic sectors: the primary sector, largely raw material extraction industries such as mining and farming; the secondary sector, involving refining, construction, and manufacturing; the tertiary sector, which deals with services (such as law and medicine) and distribution of manufactured goods; and the quaternary sector, a relatively new type of knowledge _________ focusing on technological research, design and development such as computer programming, and biochemistry.

a. ADTECH
b. ACNielsen
c. AMAX
d. Industry

4. _________ describes the situation when output from (or information about the result of) an event or phenomenon in the past will influence the same event/phenomenon in the present or future. When an event is part of a chain of cause-and-effect that forms a circuit or loop, then the event is said to 'feed back' into itself.

_________ is also a synonym for:

- _________ Signal; the information about the initial event that is the basis for subsequent modification of the event.
- _________ Loop; the causal path that leads from the initial generation of the _________ signal to the subsequent modification of the event.

_________ is a mechanism, process or signal that is looped back to control a system within itself. Such a loop is called a _________ loop.

a. 6-3-5 Brainwriting
b. 180SearchAssistant
c. Power III
d. Feedback

5. _________ is systematic determination of merit, worth, and significance of something or someone using criteria against a set of standards. _________ often is used to characterize and appraise subjects of interest in a wide range of human enterprises, including the arts, criminal justice, foundations and non-profit organizations, government, health care, and other human services.

Depending on the topic of interest, there are professional groups which look to the quality and rigor of the _________ process.

a. AMAX
b. Evaluation
c. ADTECH
d. ACNielsen

6. _________ is the realization of an application idea, model, design, specification, standard, algorithm an _________ is a realization of a technical specification or algorithm as a program, software component, or other computer system. Many _________s may exist for a given specification or standard.

a. ADTECH
b. AMAX
c. Implementation
d. ACNielsen

7. _________ is a branch of philosophy which seeks to address questions about morality, such as how a moral outcome can be achieved in a specific situation (applied _________), how moral values should be determined (normative _________), what moral values people actually abide by (descriptive _________), what the fundamental semantic, ontological, and epistemic nature of _________ or morality is (meta-_________), and how moral capacity or moral agency develops and what its nature is (moral psychology.)

Socrates was one of the first Greek philosophers to encourage both scholars and the common citizen to turn their attention from the outside world to the condition of man. In this view, Knowledge having a bearing on human life was placed highest, all other knowledge being secondary.

a. Ethics
b. ADTECH
c. ACNielsen
d. AMAX

8. _________ is a broad label that refers to any individuals or households that use goods and services generated within the economy. The concept of a _________ is used in different contexts, so that the usage and significance of the term may vary.

A _________ is a person who uses any product or service.

a. 6-3-5 Brainwriting
b. Power III
c. 180SearchAssistant
d. Consumer

9. A _________ is the space, actual or metaphorical, in which a market operates. The term is also used in a trademark law context to denote the actual consumer environment, ie. the 'real world' in which products and services are provided and consumed.

a. Marketplace
b. 6-3-5 Brainwriting
c. 180SearchAssistant
d. Power III

10. _________ networking is a method of delivering computer network services in which the participants share a portion of their own resources, such as processing power, disk storage, network bandwidth, printing facilities. Such resources are provided directly to other participants without intermediary network hosts or servers. _________ network participants are providers and consumers of network services simultaneously, which contrasts with other service models, such as traditional client-server computing.

a. 6-3-5 Brainwriting
b. 180SearchAssistant
c. Peer-to-peer
d. Power III

11. In statistics, an _________ is a term in a statistical model added when the effect of two or more variables is not simply additive. Such a term reflects that the effect of one variable depends on the values of one or more other variables.

Thus, for a response Y and two variables x_1 and x_2 an additive model would be:

$$Y = ax_1 + bx_2 + \text{error}$$

In contrast to this,

$$Y = ax_1 + bx_2 + c(x_1 \times x_2) + \text{error},$$

is an example of a model with an _________ between variables x_1 and x_2 ('error' refers to the random variable whose value by which y differs from the expected value of y.)

a. ADTECH
b. Interaction
c. ACNielsen
d. AMAX

12. _________ refer to a collection of facts usually collected as the result of experience, observation or experiment or a set of premises. This may consist of numbers, words particularly as measurements or observations of a set of variables. _________ are often viewed as a lowest level of abstraction from which information and knowledge are derived.

a. Sample size
b. Mean
c. Pearson product-moment correlation coefficient
d. Data

13. _________ is a form of communication that typically attempts to persuade potential customers to purchase or to consume more of a particular brand of product or service. 'While now central to the contemporary global economy and the reproduction of global production networks, it is only quite recently that _________ has been more than a marginal influence on patterns of sales and production. The formation of modern _________ was intimately bound up with the emergence of new forms of monopoly capitalism around the end of the 19th and beginning of the 20th century as one element in corporate strategies to create, organize and where possible control markets, especially for mass produced consumer goods.

a. ACNielsen
b. ADTECH
c. AMAX
d. Advertising

14. In finance, an _________ is a contract between a buyer and a seller that gives the buyer the right--but not the obligation--to buy or to sell a particular asset (the underlying asset) at a later day at an agreed price. In return for granting the _________, the seller collects a payment (the premium) from the buyer. A call _________ gives the buyer the right to buy the underlying asset; a put _________ gives the buyer of the _________ the right to sell the underlying asset.
a. ADTECH
b. Option
c. ACNielsen
d. AMAX

1. _________ is the set of reasons that determines one to engage in a particular behavior. The term is generally used for human _________ but, theoretically, it can be used to describe the causes for animal behavior as well
   a. Role playing
   b. Power III
   c. Motivation
   d. 180SearchAssistant

2. In economics and sociology, an _________ is any factor (financial or non-financial) that enables or motivates a particular course of action, or counts as a reason for preferring one choice to the alternatives. It is an expectation that encourages people to behave in a certain way. Since human beings are purposeful creatures, the study of _________ structures is central to the study of all economic activity (both in terms of individual decision-making and in terms of co-operation and competition within a larger institutional structure.)
   a. ADTECH
   b. ACNielsen
   c. Incentive
   d. AMAX

3. _________s are used in open sentences. For instance, in the formula x + 1 = 5, x is a _________ which represents an 'unknown' number. _________s are often represented by letters of the Roman alphabet, or those of other alphabets, such as Greek, and use other special symbols.
   a. Quantitative
   b. Personalization
   c. Book of business
   d. Variable

4. _________ is a way of expressing knowledge or belief that an event will occur or has occurred. In mathematics the concept has been given an exact meaning in _________ theory, that is used extensively in such areas of study as mathematics, statistics, finance, gambling, science, and philosophy to draw conclusions about the likelihood of potential events and the underlying mechanics of complex systems.
   a. Probability
   b. Linear regression
   c. Data
   d. Heteroskedastic

5. _________ is defined by the American _________ Association as the activity, set of institutions, and processes for creating, communicating, delivering, and exchanging offerings that have value for customers, clients, partners, and society at large. The term developed from the original meaning which referred literally to going to market, as in shopping, or going to a market to sell goods or services.

_________ practice tends to be seen as a creative industry, which includes advertising, distribution and selling.

a. Customer acquisition management
b. Marketing myopia
c. Product naming
d. Marketing

6. An _________ is a formal scheme used to promote or encourage specific actions or behavior by a specific group of people during a defined period of time. _________s are particularly used in business management to motivate employees, and in sales in order to attract and retain customers.

If programs are to be effective, all the factors that affect behavior must be recognized, including: motivation, skills, recognition, an understanding of the goals, and the ability to measure progress.

a. All commodity volume
b. Advertiser funded programming
c. Electronic retailing self-regulation program
d. Incentive program

7. _________ involves disseminating information about a product, product line, brand, or company. It is one of the four key aspects of the marketing mix. (The other three elements are product marketing, pricing, and distribution). P>_________ is generally sub-divided into two parts:

- Above the line _________: Promotion in the media (e.g. TV, radio, newspapers, Internet and Mobile Phones) in which the advertiser pays an advertising agency to place the ad
- Below the line _________: All other _________. Much of this is intended to be subtle enough for the consumer to be unaware that _________ is taking place. E.g. sponsorship, product placement, endorsements, sales _________, merchandising, direct mail, personal selling, public relations, trade shows

a. Cashmere Agency
b. Bottling lines
c. Promotion
d. Davie Brown Index

8. In accounting, _________ has a very specific meaning. It is an outflow of cash or other valuable assets from a person or company to another person or company. This outflow of cash is generally one side of a trade for products or services that have equal or better current or future value to the buyer than to the seller.

a. ADTECH
b. ACNielsen
c. Expense
d. AMAX

9. _________ is the difference between the revenues earned from and the costs associated with the customer relationship in a specified period.

According to Philip Kotler,'a profitable customer is a person, household or a company that overtime, yields a revenue stream that exceeds by an acceptable amount the company's cost stream of attracting, selling and servicing the customer'

Although _________ is nothing more than the result of applying the business concept of profit to a customer relationship, measuring the profitability of a firm's customers or customer groups can often deliver useful business insights.

Quite often a very small percentage of the firm's best customers will account for a large portion of firm profit.

a. Power III
b. 180SearchAssistant
c. Cost management
d. Customer profitability

1. In economics, business, retail, and accounting, a _________ is the value of money that has been used up to produce something, and hence is not available for use anymore. In economics, a _________ is an alternative that is given up as a result of a decision. In business, the _________ may be one of acquisition, in which case the amount of money expended to acquire it is counted as _________.

a. Transaction cost
b. Variable cost
c. Cost
d. Fixed costs

2. _________, a business term, is a measure of how products and services supplied by a company meet or surpass customer expectation. It is seen as a key performance indicator within business and is part of the four perspectives of a Balanced Scorecard.

In a competitive marketplace where businesses compete for customers, _________ is seen as a key differentiator and increasingly has become a key element of business strategy.

a. Customer base
b. Psychological pricing
c. Supplier diversity
d. Customer satisfaction

3. _________ is a costing model that identifies activities in an organization and assigns the cost of each activity resource to all products and services according to the actual consumption by each: it assigns more indirect costs (overhead) into direct costs.

In this way an organization can establish the true cost of its individual products and services for the purposes of identifying and eliminating those which are unprofitable and lowering the prices of those which are overpriced.

In a business organization, the ABC methodology assigns an organization's resource costs through activities to the products and services provided to its customers.

a. ADTECH
b. AMAX
c. ACNielsen
d. Activity-based costing

4. In marketing, customer _________, lifetime customer value (LCV), or _________ (LTV) and a new concept of 'customer life cycle management' is the present value of the future cash flows attributed to the customer relationship. Use of customer _________ as a marketing metric tends to place greater emphasis on customer service and long-term customer satisfaction, rather than on maximizing short-term sales.

Customer _________ has intuitive appeal as a marketing concept, because in theory it represents exactly how much each customer is worth in monetary terms, and therefore exactly how much a marketing department should be willing to spend to acquire each customer.

a. Lifetime value
b. Value chain
c. Sweepstakes
d. Brand infiltration

5. _________ is defined by the American _________ Association as the activity, set of institutions, and processes for creating, communicating, delivering, and exchanging offerings that have value for customers, clients, partners, and society at large. The term developed from the original meaning which referred literally to going to market, as in shopping, or going to a market to sell goods or services.

_________ practice tends to be seen as a creative industry, which includes advertising, distribution and selling.

a. Marketing myopia
b. Customer acquisition management
c. Product naming
d. Marketing

6. A personal and cultural _________ is a relative ethic _________, an assumption upon which implementation can be extrapolated. A _________ system is a set of consistent _________s and measures that is soo not true. A principle _________ is a foundation upon which other _________s and measures of integrity are based.
a. Supreme Court of the United States
b. Value
c. Package-on-Package
d. Perceptual maps

7. In cost-volume-profit analysis, a form of management accounting, _________ is the marginal profit per unit sale. It is a useful quantity in carrying out various calculations, and can be used as a measure of operating leverage.

The Total _________ is Total Revenue (TR, or Sales) minus Total Variable Cost (TVC):

TContribution margin = TR − TVC

The Unit _________ (C) is Unit Revenue (Price, P) minus Unit Variable Cost (V):

C = P - V

The _________ Ratio is the percentage of Contribution over Total Revenue, which can be calculated from the unit contribution over unit price or total contribution over Total Revenue:

$$\frac{C}{P} = \frac{P-V}{P} = \frac{\text{Unit Contribution Margin}}{\text{Price}} = \frac{\text{Total Contribution Margin}}{\text{Total Revenue}}$$

For instance, if the price is \$10 and the unit variable cost is \$2, then the unit _________ is \$8, and the _________ ratio is \$8/ \$10 = 80%.

a. Customer profitability
b. Power III
c. 180SearchAssistant
d. Contribution margin

8. In accounting, _________ has a very specific meaning. It is an outflow of cash or other valuable assets from a person or company to another person or company. This outflow of cash is generally one side of a trade for products or services that have equal or better current or future value to the buyer than to the seller.
a. ADTECH
b. AMAX
c. ACNielsen
d. Expense

9. _________ is a form of communication that typically attempts to persuade potential customers to purchase or to consume more of a particular brand of product or service. 'While now central to the contemporary global economy and the reproduction of global production networks, it is only quite recently that _________ has been more than a marginal influence on patterns of sales and production. The formation of modern _________ was intimately bound up with the emergence of new forms of monopoly capitalism around the end of the 19th and beginning of the 20th century as one element in corporate strategies to create, organize and where possible control markets, especially for mass produced consumer goods.
a. ADTECH
b. AMAX
c. ACNielsen
d. Advertising

10. _________ is one of the four aspects of promotional mix. (The other three parts of the promotional mix are advertising, personal selling, and publicity/public relations.) Media and non-media marketing communication are employed for a pre-determined, limited time to increase consumer demand, stimulate market demand or improve product availability.

a. Sales promotion
b. Merchandise
c. New Media Strategies
d. Marketing communication

11. _________ involves disseminating information about a product, product line, brand, or company. It is one of the four key aspects of the marketing mix. (The other three elements are product marketing, pricing, and distribution). P>_________ is generally sub-divided into two parts:

- Above the line _________: Promotion in the media (e.g. TV, radio, newspapers, Internet and Mobile Phones) in which the advertiser pays an advertising agency to place the ad
- Below the line _________: All other _________. Much of this is intended to be subtle enough for the consumer to be unaware that _________ is taking place. E.g. sponsorship, product placement, endorsements, sales _________, merchandising, direct mail, personal selling, public relations, trade shows

a. Promotion
b. Cashmere Agency
c. Davie Brown Index
d. Bottling lines

12. _________ operations or facilities are commonly called 'distribution centers'. '_________' is the term generally used to describe the process or the work flow associated with the picking, packing and delivery of the packed item(s) to a shipping carrier.

a. AMAX
b. ADTECH
c. ACNielsen
d. Order processing

13. _________ is a retail channel for the distribution of goods and services. At a basic level it may be defined as marketing and selling products, direct to consumers away from a fixed retail location. Sales are typically made through party plan, one to one demonstrations, and other personal contact arrangements.

a. Direct selling
b. 180SearchAssistant
c. 6-3-5 Brainwriting
d. Power III

14. In economics and sociology, an _________ is any factor (financial or non-financial) that enables or motivates a particular course of action, or counts as a reason for preferring one choice to the alternatives. It is an expectation that encourages people to behave in a certain way. Since human beings are purposeful creatures, the study of _________ structures is central to the study of all economic activity (both in terms of individual decision-making and in terms of co-operation and competition within a larger institutional structure.)

a. Incentive
b. AMAX
c. ACNielsen
d. ADTECH

15. In economics, _________ are business expenses that are not dependent on the activities of the business They tend to be time-related, such as salaries or rents being paid per month. This is in contrast to variable costs, which are volume-related (and are paid per quantity.)

In management accounting, _________ are defined as expenses that do not change in proportion to the activity of a business, within the relevant period or scale of production.

a. Transaction cost
b. Marginal cost
c. Variable cost
d. Fixed costs

1. _________ is a social psychology theory developed by Fritz Heider, Harold Kelley, Edward E. Jones, and Lee Ross.

The theory is concerned with the ways in which people explain (or attribute) the behavior of others or themselves (self-attribution) with something else. It explores how individuals 'attribute' causes to events and how this cognitive perception affects their usefulness in an organization.

a. ADTECH
b. AMAX
c. ACNielsen
d. Attribution theory

2. _________ is the set of reasons that determines one to engage in a particular behavior. The term is generally used for human _________ but, theoretically, it can be used to describe the causes for animal behavior as well

a. Power III
b. Role playing
c. 180SearchAssistant
d. Motivation

3. _________s are used in open sentences. For instance, in the formula x + 1 = 5, x is a _________ which represents an 'unknown' number. _________s are often represented by letters of the Roman alphabet, or those of other alphabets, such as Greek, and use other special symbols.

a. Variable
b. Book of business
c. Personalization
d. Quantitative

4. _________ is systematic determination of merit, worth, and significance of something or someone using criteria against a set of standards. _________ often is used to characterize and appraise subjects of interest in a wide range of human enterprises, including the arts, criminal justice, foundations and non-profit organizations, government, health care, and other human services.

Depending on the topic of interest, there are professional groups which look to the quality and rigor of the _________ process.

a. ADTECH
b. ACNielsen
c. AMAX
d. Evaluation

5. _________ is a standard point of view or personal prejudice. especially when the tendency interferes with the ability to be impartial, unprejudiced, or objective. The term _________ed is used to describe an action, judgment, or other outcome influenced by a prejudged perspective.

a. Bias
b. 6-3-5 Brainwriting
c. Power III
d. 180SearchAssistant

6. In accounting, _________ has a very specific meaning. It is an outflow of cash or other valuable assets from a person or company to another person or company. This outflow of cash is generally one side of a trade for products or services that have equal or better current or future value to the buyer than to the seller.

a. ACNielsen
b. AMAX
c. ADTECH
d. Expense

7. In economics, business, retail, and accounting, a _________ is the value of money that has been used up to produce something, and hence is not available for use anymore. In economics, a _________ is an alternative that is given up as a result of a decision. In business, the _________ may be one of acquisition, in which case the amount of money expended to acquire it is counted as _________.

a. Cost
b. Variable cost
c. Transaction cost
d. Fixed costs

8. In mathematics, an _________, or central tendency of a data set refers to a measure of the 'middle' or 'expected' value of the data set. There are many different descriptive statistics that can be chosen as a measurement of the central tendency of the data items.

An _________ is a single value that is meant to typify a list of values.

a. ADTECH
b. AMAX
c. ACNielsen
d. Average

9. _________ in economics refers to metrics and measures of output from production processes, per unit of input. Labor _________, for example, is typically measured as a ratio of output per labor-hour, an input. _________ may be conceived of as a metrics of the technical or engineering efficiency of production.

a. Value engineering
b. 180SearchAssistant
c. Power III
d. Productivity

10. A _________ attribute is one that exists in a range of magnitudes, and can therefore be measured. Measurements of any particular _________ property are expressed as a specific quantity, referred to as a unit, multiplied by a number. Examples of physical quantities are distance, mass, and time.

a. Lifestyle city
b. Dolly Dimples
c. BeyondROI
d. Quantitative

11. _________ is a technical term used in management science popularized by Joseph M. Juran

He defined an internal and external customers as anyone affected by the product or by the process used to produce the product, in the context of quality management. _________s may play the role as supplier, processer, and customer in the sequence of product development.

He claimed that the organization must understand and identify both internal and external customers and their needs.

a. AMAX
b. ADTECH
c. ACNielsen
d. Internal customer

12. _________ describes the situation when output from (or information about the result of) an event or phenomenon in the past will influence the same event/phenomenon in the present or future. When an event is part of a chain of cause-and-effect that forms a circuit or loop, then the event is said to 'feed back' into itself.

_________ is also a synonym for:

- _________ Signal; the information about the initial event that is the basis for subsequent modification of the event.
- _________ Loop; the causal path that leads from the initial generation of the _________ signal to the subsequent modification of the event.

_________ is a mechanism, process or signal that is looped back to control a system within itself. Such a loop is called a _________ loop.

a. 6-3-5 Brainwriting
b. 180SearchAssistant
c. Power III
d. Feedback

Chapter 1

1. d	2. d	3. a	4. d	5. a	6. d	7. c	8. a	9. d	10. a
11. d	12. d	13. b	14. d	15. b	16. d	17. d	18. d	19. d	20. d
21. c	22. c	23. b	24. b	25. c	26. b	27. a	28. d	29. d	30. c
31. d	32. d	33. c	34. d	35. c	36. a	37. c	38. b	39. d	40. b
41. b	42. c	43. d	44. d	45. d	46. a	47. c	48. c	49. d	50. b
51. b	52. a	53. d	54. a	55. b	56. d	57. c	58. a	59. d	60. b

Chapter 2

1. d	2. c	3. d	4. c	5. b	6. a	7. d	8. a	9. d	10. d
11. d	12. b	13. d	14. a	15. a	16. a	17. d	18. d	19. a	20. d
21. d	22. d	23. a	24. b	25. d	26. c	27. d	28. d	29. b	30. d
31. d	32. d	33. a	34. d	35. a	36. d	37. d	38. a	39. d	40. d
41. c	42. d	43. c	44. d						

Chapter 3

1. a	2. c	3. b	4. b	5. b	6. d	7. c	8. d	9. b	10. a
11. d	12. a	13. d	14. d	15. d	16. d	17. c	18. d	19. d	20. c
21. c	22. c	23. c	24. d	25. a	26. c	27. a	28. b	29. a	30. c
31. b	32. d	33. d	34. d	35. b	36. d	37. c	38. b	39. d	40. a
41. d	42. b	43. a	44. d	45. d	46. a	47. c	48. c	49. d	50. a
51. b	52. d	53. d							

Chapter 4

1. d	2. d	3. d	4. a	5. a	6. c	7. b	8. c	9. c	10. b
11. d	12. b	13. b	14. d	15. d	16. d	17. b	18. c		

Chapter 5

1. d	2. b	3. b	4. d	5. d	6. b	7. d	8. d	9. a	10. c
11. d	12. d	13. d	14. d	15. d	16. d	17. c	18. a	19. c	20. d
21. a	22. d	23. c	24. d	25. c	26. d				

Chapter 6

1. a	2. d	3. d	4. c	5. d	6. a	7. d	8. d	9. a	10. a
11. c	12. d	13. d	14. a	15. d	16. a				

Chapter 7

1. d	2. d	3. b	4. d	5. d	6. d	7. d	8. d	9. c	10. b
11. d									

Chapter 8

1. d	2. d	3. d	4. d	5. d	6. b	7. b	8. c	9. c	10. b
11. d	12. b	13. d	14. c	15. b	16. d	17. d	18. a	19. b	20. d
21. b									

Chapter 9

1. d	2. a	3. d	4. b	5. d	6. a	7. a	8. a	9. a	10. d
11. a	12. a	13. a	14. b	15. d	16. a	17. a			

Chapter 10

1. d	2. b	3. d	4. d	5. b	6. c	7. a	8. d	9. a	10. c
11. b	12. d	13. d	14. b						

Chapter 11

1. c	2. c	3. d	4. a	5. d	6. d	7. c	8. c	9. d

Chapter 12

1. c	2. d	3. d	4. a	5. d	6. b	7. d	8. d	9. d	10. a
11. a	12. d	13. a	14. a	15. d					

Chapter 13

1. d	2. d	3. a	4. d	5. a	6. d	7. a	8. d	9. d	10. d
11. d	12. d								

www.ingramcontent.com/pod-product-compliance
Lightning Source LLC
Chambersburg PA
CBHW081845230426
43669CB00018B/2828